The Story of
ELI WHITNEY

{ Invention and Progress
in the Young Nation }

by Jean Lee Latham

Illustrated by FRITZ KREDEL

Sonlight Curriculum Ltd.

Cover illustration by Drew Thurston, copyright 2000 by Sonlight Curriculum, Ltd.

Printed in the United States of America.

First Sonlight Curriculum, Ltd. Edition, 2000.

ISBN 1-887840-42-7
ISBN 978-1-887840-42-2
For a catalog of Sonlight Curriculum materials for the home school, write:

Sonlight Curriculum, Ltd.
8042 South Grant Way
Littleton, CO 80122-2705
USA

Or e-mail: catalog@sonlight.com

Contents

The Promise

⊞ ELI TURNED HIS FATHER'S cattle into the stony Massachusetts pasture. He watched them scatter as they began to graze. It was almost school time. Eli sighed. It wasn't much fun to be a big boy of nine and have to read with little eight-year-olds. Girls, even. Of course, he could beat them ciphering. But no one said anything about that; no one but Hiram Wedge, the peddler.

Eli climbed the stony hill and stood on his favorite lookout rock. He shaded his eyes from the April sun and stared down the muddy road toward Worchester.

5

"I'm silly," he told himself. "Hiram Wedge and his peddler's wagon won't be coming up the road for weeks. Hiram said he was going clear to Virginia this trip."

Yes, it would be a long time before he'd see Hiram take off his three-cornered hat and wave. It would be a long time before he'd see Hiram's red hair blazing in the sun.

Far down the road, a man on horseback topped the rise of a hill. Eli watched him. Whew! He was riding like the wind! You'd think a whole tribe of Indians were after him.

Eli said, "That's silly, too." Indians weren't on the warpath in Massachusetts now. This was the humdrum year of 1775. All the excitement was over. "I wish I'd been born sooner. Then I'd have fought in the French and Indian War. I'd be a hero. No one has a chance to be a hero now—no one but Tom Cook."

Tom Cook! The highwayman of West-borough! People said he robbed the rich to help the poor. Eli remembered the time he told his father he'd like to be another Tom Cook. He wouldn't say that again! Not to his father. Grownups didn't seem to understand about Tom Cook.

Hiram Wedge might. Hiram understood

a lot of things. Who knew? Maybe Hiram Wedge was a highwayman, too. He looked like some kind of hero—tall and strong and always ready to laugh.

"The next time I see Hiram," Eli thought, "I'll tell him I'm going to be a highwayman. When I'm sixteen. Or fourteen. Why not when I'm twelve? Father's always talking about when he was twelve. *When I was twelve, I was doing a man's work.* That's what he says. So why can't I be doing a man's work when I'm twelve? A highwayman's work. Yes, sir, the next time I see Hiram . . ."

Eli gulped and stared toward the road. The galloping horseman took off his hat and waved. His red hair blazed in the sun. It was Hiram! Hiram, without his peddler's wagon!

Eli answered the wave and started down the hill, jumping over stones, digging his heels into the muddy ground. "I'm right! Hiram is a highwayman! He robs the rich to help the poor! Now the rich are chasing him! He wants me to hide him! He knows I'm his friend!"

Hiram was very close now. Eli could hear the *slotch slotch* of the horse's hooves, pulling out of the mud. He could see the musket across Hiram's saddle. All these years Hiram must have kept the musket hidden in his wagon. At night, he brought out the musket; he waited in the dark for a stagecoach; he stepped from the shadows. "Halt! Give up your gold! I rob the rich to help the poor!"

Eli reached the road and stood panting. Hiram's horse reared, snorted, and stopped. Hiram swung down from his saddle.

"I hoped I'd see you, lad. Lucky you were on the hill. I wouldn't have had time to hunt for you."

The rich were after Hiram! Eli said, "But I can hide you. I know where there's a cave."

Hiram blinked. "What are you talking about?"

Eli said, "I thought maybe you were another Tom Cook. When I saw you riding so fast . . ."

Hiram threw back his head and laughed. "Bless you, lad. I'm nothing but Hiram Wedge, Yankee peddler—late of Massachusetts—*and now of America.*"

Eli had a feeling Hiram's eyes were looking at him and seeing something else. "Hiram, where's your wagon?"

Hiram waved toward the south. "Clear

back in Virginia. Old fellow I know said he'd
take care of it for me until . . ." Hiram
grinned. "I'm forgetting why I wanted to
see you." He opened his saddlebag. "Remember
that new knife I had? The pocketknife
with two blades?" He laid the knife in Eli's
hand. "It's for you, lad."

"To keep? But why?"

Hiram's fingers gripped Eli's shoulder. "Because
I want you to remember Hiram Wedge.
I want you to remember I said that some day
you'll be a great man."

Eli felt a hot flush crawling from his chest
to his hair. "I don't see how you can tell
that. Nobody else thinks I'll amount to anything.
Here I am, going on ten. Almost a
man. I'm reading with little eight-year-olds.
Girls, even."

"How about ciphering?" Hiram asked.
"Who's fastest there? How about whittling?
Who can carve better than you?"

Eli said, "But that's easy. I'm just good
at easy things. Father says I'm not worth
my salt around the farm. He says a six-year-old
is more dependable about doing chores
than I am. You know his shop, where he
mends things?"

Hiram nodded.

"When I'm in there, tinkering, I forget my chores. It's true, Hiram. I'm not worth my salt. I'm—nobody."

Hiram said, "Every great man was yesterday's nobody. Remember that, Eli. Even if I never see you again."

"But why won't I see you again? What's wrong?"

"Lad, it's coming—war," answered the peddler.

"With the Indians?" Eli's eyes widened.

"No. With the British. King George is starving us out. He's ruining our trade so we can't earn money. He's taking what money we do have in taxes." Hiram shook his head. "And to think it took a Virginian to make me understand! Me—Massachusetts born and bred—and it took a Virginian to make me know the truth."

Hiram hooked his elbow over the pommel of his saddle. Eli perched on a stump to listen. No one else in the world could tell stories like Hiram!

"I was down in Richmond the other day, Eli. That's a town in Virginia. I was passing a church. Some kind of meeting was going on. I didn't know what. I guess I didn't care what. All at once, a speaker's voice got louder. I could hear him plain as you can hear me, now. He said, 'The distinctions between Virginians, Pennsylvanians, New Yorkers, and New Englanders are no more. I am not a Virginian, but an American.' "

"What did he mean?"

"Well, *distinction* means *difference*—the ways we are not alike; he meant we aren't thirteen separate colonies; we're all one."

Eli said, "But how can New Englanders be the same as Virginians? Father says Virginians are 'godless cavaliers.' "

Hiram nodded. "I know, lad. We've spent about a hundred and fifty years thinking about our differences. We're going to have to learn to be one people. Not New Englanders. Not Virginians. Just Americans."

Eli shook his head slowly. "I don't think father will."

Hiram searched in his saddlebag and found a piece of paper. "Here, lad, I wrote it down for you. What he said about being an American. And the last thing I heard him say." Hiram read: " 'Is life so dear or peace so sweet, as to be purchased at the price of chains and slavery? Forbid it, Almighty God! I know not what course others may take, but as for me, give me liberty or give me death!' "

Eli tried to say something, but he couldn't swallow the lump in his throat.

Hiram gave him the paper. "It's for you, lad."

Eli said, "I'm going to learn it by heart."

Hiram said, "Good. The day will come when every schoolboy will know those words. You'll be one of the first."

"Who said it, Hiram?"

"A Virginia lawyer," the peddler answered. "Fellow by the name of Patrick Henry." Hiram turned to his saddle. "Well, this isn't getting to Boston. I've got to get the musket fixed, too. A broken hammer. It'll take me half a day, like as not."

Eli said, "I can help you, Hiram! There's a musket here with a split barrel. But the hammer's all right. We'll put that hammer in your musket and . . ."

Hiram shook his head. "It wouldn't fit. We don't turn out muskets, one after the other, like chair legs or fence posts. Each musket's handmade. Every piece of it fits that musket and no other. If you had two dozen muskets here, you couldn't find a hammer to fit mine."

Eli said. "That's too bad."

Hiram grinned. "I know. But it's the nature of muskets." He swung into his saddle. "Well, good-by, lad. I'm off to Boston."

"Where will you go in Boston?"

Hiram's eyes got that seeing-through-you look again. "First, there's a silversmith in Boston I want to talk to. He knows what's coming. He tried to tell me. I was too busy peddling my wares to listen. First, I'll see him. Then I'll shoulder my musket, fall in, and start drilling." Hiram picked up his reins. "Giddap."

Eli ran after him. "Hiram!"

Hiram pulled up his horse and turned. "Yes, lad?"

"Be sure to come back. You're my best friend. If you didn't come back, I don't know what I'd do."

Hiram smiled. "You're going to be a great man, Eli. You'll keep on till you are. All your life, you'll keep on keeping on." Hiram lifted his hat. His red hair glinted in the sun. He wheeled his horse.

"But Hiram!"

Hiram stopped again. "Yes, lad?"

"You'll have to come back," Eli said earnestly. "I'll want to know what the silversmith says."

Hiram threw back his head and laughed. "I'll see that you hear about that!" He rode away. The *slotch slotch* of his horse's hooves faded.

Eli looked after him. "Now I'll be watching the road from Boston."

It was early June when Eli saw a rider

coming on the road from Boston. The man reined his horse and called to Eli. "Are you Eli Whitney?"

"Yes, sir."

The stranger swung from his horse and opened a saddlebag. "Then I've a letter for you."

"A letter?" Eli said. "It must be for my father. We have the same name."

The man said, "I think it's for you." He read the address. " 'Eli Whitney. Aged Nine. The Whitney Farm. Westborough. Massachusetts.' " He gave the letter to Eli—a paper folded and sealed with a circle of wax.

Eli recognized the handwriting. "It's from Hiram Wedge. He's my best friend!"

"That's so, lad?" The man laid his hand on Eli's shoulder.

Eli loosened the seal, opened his letter, and read:

Boston, April 18, 1775

DEAR ELI,

I promised to let you know what the silver smith said. He wasn't home when I got here tonight. They said he was out on an errand. If I see him later, I'll let you know what he says. Did I tell you his name? It's Paul Revere.

Your friend,

HIRAM WEDGE

Eli said, "He wrote me a letter because he promised! That day he went to Boston. When his musket had a broken hammer. He said he'd get a new hammer, and then he'd 'fall in and start drilling.' "

The man looked away. "I guess the new hammer wasn't very good," he said slowly. "His musket had a broken hammer when I found him."

Eli's mouth felt dry. "What do you mean?"

"Hiram Wedge died at Bunker Hill. With a broken musket in his hands. I found the letter on his body." The stranger's fingers gripped Eli's shoulder. "I'm sorry, lad." He swung into his saddle, jerked the reins, shouted "giddap" to his horse, and rode off.

Stumbling, Eli climbed the stony hill to his lookout rock. He stared out the road toward Boston. It seemed that Hiram was there beside him. Hiram's hand on his shoulder. Hiram's voice saying, "You'll be a great man, Eli. You keep on till you are."

Eli whispered, "I will, Hiram. No matter what! I'll keep on keeping on!"

The Long Road

⟐ ELI STOPPED WEEDING AND wiped the sweat off his forehead with the back of his hand. Weeds! The hotter it was, the faster they grew. But he was twelve now. Big enough to do a man's work. He'd hurry with the weeding. Then, while his father was away on the trip, he'd have time to finish his surprise.

Out of the tail of his eye, Eli saw his father climb on Dolly's back and start down the lane.

Eli counted to a hundred, dusted the dirt from his hands on his trousers, and hurried to the shop. He brought some pieces of wood

17

from a hiding place behind a pile of lumber. Nobody else in Westborough had ever made a fiddle. When his father saw this . . .

"I'll finish the weeding later," he told himself, "when the fiddle's done."

It was some three days later—or maybe four—he'd rather lost track of the time. Eli tuned the fiddle and tightened the bow. The shop door slammed open. His father glared down at him. Oh, no! It couldn't be a whole week later!

"Eli! Can't I depend on you for anything? You haven't touched that weeding since . . . What's this?" He snatched the fiddle from Eli's hands. For a moment, Eli thought his father would smash it.

But just then, Jasper Kelly, a neighbor, meandered into the shop with a broken wheel. "Glad you're back, Mr. Whitney. This wheel—" He stopped. "Bless me! I didn't know you could make a fiddle." Jasper took the fiddle, twanged the strings with his thumb. "Yes, sir, it's all right."

His father's voice was flat. "I didn't make it."

Jasper said, "No? Well, I didn't think anyone in these parts could make a fiddle. Where'd you get it?"

"Well, Eli?" His father looked stern.
Eli gulped. "I made it."

Jasper said, "Well!" He rumpled Eli's hair. "Mr. Whitney, you've got a young mechanic! Yes, sir! A man could be proud of that work!"

A man's work! That's what Jasper meant! In a moment, his father would smile and say—

But Mr. Whitney frowned. "I'm not raising Eli to be a mechanic. He's my first-born. He'll have the chance I didn't have. Go to college. Follow a profession." Eli's father smiled now. "You'll like that, won't you, Eli? Study hard, go to Yale, be a teacher or a lawyer?"

Eli wished he could say "Yes," so his father would keep smiling. But he shook his head. "No, Father. I'm not good at books. Only at ciphering."

Jasper nodded. "A mechanic through and through! I tell you, that fiddle is remarkable for a boy of twelve!"

Mr. Whitney stopped smiling. "Fiddling is a waste of time."

No . . . a fiddle wasn't a man's work. Eli understood he'd have to do better than that. Something worth doing.

When he was fourteen, Eli found something worth doing. His stepmother had lost a pin and was fussing about it.

"I paid seven shillings for a dozen pins! And now I've lost one! Goodness knows when I'll get more! Nothing comes from England now."

His father said, "Humph. If you'd lost a nail, I'd worry more. If nails get much scarcer, we'll be doing like they did in the old days. I've heard tell nails were so scarce then, that when a man moved, he'd burn down his house to get back his nails."

Nails! They were the thing!

Eli spent his spare time at Mr. Bixler's forge. He lost count of how many iron rods he used before he could heat one just right, make a nail, and head and point it. Finally, he had a dozen nails that suited him.

Even Mr. Bixler nodded. "That's good deft work, Eli. A man could be proud of those nails."

A man's work! Eli took the nails home.

His father said, "Humph." Eli knew he was still thinking about college, and having his son study a profession.

But men bought the nails. They paid a good price for them. Eli got so busy he had to hire a man to help him. "This is a man's work," he told himself. "People will come from further and further away. I'll get more helpers. Some day I'll . . ."

But the war ended. Goods came from England again. Nobody wanted handmade nails. They cost too much.

Eli was eighteen when he said, "Father, I know now you were right. I'm going to Yale."

His father said, "Humph. Too late for that now. Most boys are through college when they're eighteen."

"I know." Eli had thought about that. "I'll be older when I go."

His father snapped, "You can't go. There's no money to help you now."

"I'll earn my way. They want a teacher over at Grafton. They'll pay seven dollars a month and board." He knew what his father was thinking. "I know I wasn't much of a scholar. Things were hard for me. Maybe that will help me to help the children when it's hard for them."

His father sighed. "Maybe you would make a good teacher, Eli. You're patient. Teach if you want to. But don't think about college, son. It's too late."

"I'll teach in the winter and study in the summer to get ready for college."

His father said, "Humph."

After five years, he bellowed, "Eli! How much longer are you going to keep this up?"

Eli said, "Until I have saved enough money to go to college."

Mr. Whitney rumpled his hair and frowned. "Then go," he said. "When you run out of money, I'll lend you some."

"But where will you get it?" Eli knew that times were hard.

"I'll mortgage the farm. Go on down to New Haven. If you can pass the examinations, get started. You'll be an old man when you finish, now!"

"Thank you. The spring term opens the end of April. I'll try to be ready then."

*   *   *

Eli closed the Latin book, and leaned his head on his hands. It wasn't any use. He wasn't a scholar. The longer he studied, the more he forgot. When he faced President Stiles of Yale College tomorrow, he'd probably forget everything he ever knew.

"I'll walk a while," he decided. "Then I can study some more tonight."

An hour later he stood on the red cliffs

above Mill River and looked down on New Haven, at the white sails in the harbor. He stared down at the Green, at Yale College. Fourteen years ago, a little boy had stood on another rock, and made a promise. "I seem to be keeping on," Eli thought, "but it's a long road."

Behind him, a voice called, "Hello, there!"

Eli turned and smiled down at two boys. Maybe all boys liked a lookout rock, where they could stand and view the world. These two weren't much older than he'd been when he first had a lookout rock.

One youngster offered his hand. "I'm Charles Chauncey. And he is Tom Savage. He's a stranger in New Haven. I'm showing him the sights. Are you a stranger, too?"

"Yes, I'm a stranger, too. I'm Eli Whitney."

"Then I'll show you the sights, too. What's that you're making?"

Eli looked down at his hands. He grinned. He hadn't even noticed that he was whittling. He gave the slim bit of carving to Charles. "See if you can tell what it is."

Charles said, "Why, it's a musket. Look, Tom! A tiny musket! It's perfect!"

Eli said, "No. Not perfect. It has a broken hammer. I saw a musket like that once. But I'll make you a perfect one if you like. I'll make one for each of you."

Tom said, "That will be fine, sir." He spoke in a soft southern drawl. "Do you always carry wood in your pockets, sir?"

Eli said, "I seem to." He began to whittle. The boys watched, silent, big-eyed.

Charles said, "Maybe we can show you some more sights tomorrow. Maybe you'll have your knife again."

Eli shook his head. "Tomorrow, I'm afraid I'll be too busy for whittling. I have to see President Stiles."

Charles smiled. "Are you going to be one of our tutors? I hope so!"

"Where are you in school?" Eli asked.

Charles said, "In Yale College. We both are. I passed my examinations last year. But

I was only ten. My father thought I ought to wait till this year to enter. Are you going to be one of our tutors?"

For a moment, Eli didn't answer. Then he smiled. He might as well get used to this now. "No, Charles. I'm going to be one of your classmates—if I pass my examinations tomorrow. I'm twenty-three, and just entering Yale."

Finally Tom Savage broke the silence. "Well, sir, you certainly are clever with your hands."

Two days later, Eli met the boys on the Green. Between them was a husky-looking man with a weatherbeaten face and a quick grin.

Tom said, "Congratulations, Mr. Whitney."

Charles said, "We were just hunting for you. This is Amos Hoyt. He's in our class."

Over the heads of the boys, Amos winked at Eli. "And I'm twenty-seven," he said.

Eli grinned. Very polite lads, young Charles and Tom. They must have spent quite a bit of time finding Amos. The one man in the class who was older than Eli.

In a Strange Land

☞ THE AUTUMN DAY THEY GRAD-
uated from Yale, Amos Hoyt and Eli climbed
the red cliffs above Mill River together.

Amos said, "You must like this spot."

Eli nodded. "I said hello to New Haven
here; I thought I'd say good-by here, too."

"You're determined to go to Georgia," Amos
asked, "and take that job of tutoring?"

"Yes."

"It's double work—trying to teach and read
law, too."

"I have to," Eli said. "I'm in debt. I can't
wait three years to start earning money. It'll

26

be at least that long before I can pass my examinations to be a lawyer."

"Well, if you're bent on going, here's something." Amos reached in his pocket. "Notice of a boat sailing for Savannah. I got it from a New York paper."

Eli read the scrap of paper:

> For Savannah, Georgia
> The brigantine, *Mary*
> Benjamin Lowe, Commander.
> Sails in fourteen days.

He asked, "When did you get it, Amos?"

"Just a day or two ago. The boat hasn't gone yet."

Eli said, "The stagecoach is probably faster. It takes only a little over two weeks."

Amos shook his head. "I heard of a man who went from Philadelphia to Baltimore by stage. It took him five days. Five days on those backless board benches. That was enough. He made the trip back by boat."

Eli pocketed the notice. Maybe the boat was better, even if it took longer. He'd have his books with him. He could set himself a stint of reading to do every day. "I'll write to Georgia tonight—tell Mr. Baldwin I'll come that way."

A few days later, when the brigantine,

Mary, sailed for Savannah, Eli was on board. He picked his way along the cluttered deck, and sat on a packing box. This was better than the confusion below deck.

For a moment he looked at the heavy law book in his hands. Twenty-six, and just through college! It would be three years yet before he'd even begin to amount to anything.

Well, Patrick Henry hadn't amounted to much when he was young. He'd failed at a lot of things. Then he made a great speech. Yesterday's nobody; tomorrow's great man.

What did it take, Eli wondered, to turn yesterday's nobody into a great man? How did you happen to do something your country would never forget? Maybe your country had to need you. Maybe that need jerked you out of yourself and made you do more than you ever knew you could.

Eli sighed. Maybe he'd been born too late to set the world on fire. He'd been too young for the French and Indian War; too young for the Revolution. His classmates at Yale had often talked about how they were born too late for greatness.

He remembered the excitement at Yale when news came of the French Revolution. Excitement had swept through the college, and pride, too. We—the youngest of all the nations—had led the way! Now the French were following our lead, struggling against the power of a king, just as we had struggled.

He remembered the students who wished they were rich enough to raise an army and go to help the downtrodden people of France, just as Lafayette had helped us. They didn't know just what the struggle was all about, but they were sure the people were right and the king was wrong. And, besides, there was a chance for greatness, overseas. Our struggle was over. There was nothing for Americans now but the humdrum of everyday life.

Well, one thing sure, he couldn't go to France. Eli opened his book. He was late starting, and would have to hustle to catch up. If he read ten hours a day, all the way to Savannah . . .

A voice behind him said, "You're Eli Whitney, aren't you? Going to Georgia as a tutor?"

Who in the name of sense knew he was on board? And knew that much about him? Eli's glance traveled from the man's shining buckles and white silk hose up to his face. He saw a thin, tense face, with lines between the eyes. But the stranger was smiling now.

"Yes, I'm Whitney." Eli rose slowly to his

feet and stood towering over the other man. "I'm Phineas Miller. Yale, Class of '85. I went to Georgia as a tutor, myself. At Mulberry Grove. Now I manage the plantation. Come along with me. There's someone on board you must meet."

Eli said, "I'm sorry, but I've set myself a stint of reading to do. Perhaps later."

Phineas Miller laughed. "You might as well come; the general's widow never takes 'no' for an answer."

"General . . . Mulberry Grove. . . ." Something clicked in Eli's memory. Mulberry Grove was the name of a plantation. The state of Georgia had given it to General Greene. General Nathanael Greene! Next to Washington, the greatest general of them all!

Eli slapped his book shut. "I'll be delighted to meet Madame Greene." He followed Phineas Miller, trying to imagine what the general's widow would be like. Probably an old woman, with a sad, stern face.

Phineas led the way to a young-looking woman with sparkling eyes. "I found him, Catherine," he said.

Catherine Greene smiled up at Eli. "I heard you would be the tallest man on board."

Her voice had a chuckle running through it. "You see, I've heard of you. I have friends in New Haven. How nice you're making the trip to Savannah with us. You'll have to stop a while at Mulberry Grove before you start your tutoring."

Eli stared in blank amazement. Hiram used to tell him about the hospitality of planters in the South. But General Greene's widow couldn't be asking a stranger to visit her.

Madame Greene seemed not to notice Eli's surprise. "I'm sure you'll enjoy a few weeks at Mulberry Grove. And I know we'll enjoy having you."

A few weeks! Eli finally found his tongue. "You're very kind, Madame Greene. But I don't have time to visit now. I must keep working. You see, I'm very late starting."

Catherine Greene cocked her pretty head and smiled up at him. "New England born and bred! Well, so am I, but I've learned there's more to life than hustle and bustle! Well, then, sit down, and we'll tell you all about Georgia."

Eli tried to explain about his stint of reading. She waved that aside. "Nonsense, Mr. Whitney. It's much more important for you to hear about Georgia. You know, when you get there, you'll be a stranger in a strange land."

A stranger in a strange land. Eli thought of that as the boat turned into the Savannah River and sailed toward the city of Savannah. Up north, it was autumn. The air was crisp. Here the muggy heat made you tired before you moved. Up north, the trees were gold and red and tawny brown. Here, great gnarled green trees dripped something gray called Spanish moss.

The boat docked in Savannah. Laughing friends surrounded Catherine Greene and Phineas Miller. They moved away in the middle of a throng.

Eli might have been with them if he had not refused the invitation to visit Mulberry Grove. He almost ran after them, calling, "Wait! Wait! I've changed my mind!"

He left the boat slowly, feeling very much alone among strangers. Then a slender young man with bright blue eyes approached him. "Are you by any chance Mr. Whitney, sir?"

How in the world did anyone in Georgia know he'd be on the boat? Then he remembered he had written to Mr. Baldwin. Someone had come to meet him.

The heavy lump in Eli's chest felt lighter. "Yes, I'm Whitney." He smiled and took the note the young man handed him. He was still smiling when he opened it.

The words on the paper seemed to crawl and dance in the heat. Eli shut his eyes, opened them, and tried again to read. There'd been a mistake, the note said, a mistake in the pay offered him. He'd get only half what he had expected.

Eli didn't know whether the sick feeling in the pit of his stomach was anger, disappointment, or fear. What could he do? Work his way back to New Haven on the boat? Try to get a job there, where he was known?

The young man was waiting. Eli said, "Tell Mr. Baldwin I'll get in touch with him later."

The young man bowed and was gone.

Eli was alone in the jostling throng. Nine years! Nine years since he'd decided to go to college and make something of his life. Five years of teaching all winter and going to school all summer. Four years at Yale. And now . . . this. He stood there, numb among the laughing strangers who hurried by, unheeding. He stood quite still, making neat, even folds in the letter.

The Challenge

⟐ "WHAT IS IT, ELI? BAD NEWS?"

Eli whirled. Catherine Greene and Phineas Miller stood behind him. "I thought you'd gone."

Madame Greene said, "We started. Then we saw you standing here. You know, you do tower head and shoulders over everyone. What is it? Bad news?"

Eli gave her the letter.

She scanned the page. "Not bad news at all. Now, you won't have to waste time tutoring. You shall come to Mulberry Grove. You'll have all your time to read law."

34

Eli said, "I have my living to earn. I can't just—"

She said, "At least you can visit us a while. Till we think of something." Her eyes danced as they measured Eli's height. "I think you should have the rose room. General Washington slept there when he visited Mulberry Grove last year. There's a very long bed."

Numb with bewilderment, Eli followed to the boat which was to take them up river to Mulberry Grove. The Negro oarsmen greeted Catherine Greene.

One said, "We got company, ma'am. Major Bainbridge and some friends."

She said, "Wonderful, Ben! We'll have a dance. You'll like that, won't you? And so will Jim. He'll fiddle all night and be late getting to the field in the morning."

Ben threw back his head and laughed. "Yes, ma'am!"

Eli blinked. What kind of world was this? Where visitors came to see a hostess who wasn't home? Where a servant was excused from honest toil because he'd played a fiddle the night before? A strange world!

"I suppose I'll have to see it to understand it," Eli thought.

But after a week he still couldn't understand Mulberry Grove. He could understand the difference in houses. Up north, New Englanders built to escape the cold. The rooms huddled around the chimney. The kitchen was the center of the home. At Mulberry Grove, the big house seemed stretched out to catch the breeze. Long verandas shaded it from the sun. The kitchen was banished to another building. Southerners built to escape the heat.

He could understand the difference in crops. What else would they grow in that swampy land but rice? They had to grow a crop that liked to get its feet wet.

But he couldn't understand Catherine Greene. How could she expect him to stay on at Mulberry Grove and give nothing in return? Didn't she know he must pay his way? Where he came from, even a child was supposed to be worth his salt.

He felt a little better one day when he had a chance to mend a watch for her. But it embarrassed him when she was so grateful.

"It's wonderful, Eli! Here, I thought I'd have to send it to England to have it fixed."

Eli said, "It's nothing. I was about so high the first time I took my father's watch apart and put it back together. I remember, I played sick and stayed home from meeting to get a chance to do it."

"When you were just a child? Eli, you're amazing!" Catharine Greene smiled.

Eli couldn't think of an answer. Silent, he watched her hands move deftly over her embroidery frame. He wished he could make her understand, that he could tell her how kind she was. He wished he knew how to talk to a woman. But he didn't. If he tried, he'd be sure to say the wrong thing.

Then, to his horror, he heard himself say, "You're the kindest person I've ever known, except a Yankee peddler. You . . ." He stopped, and hunted wildly for words to apologize.

But Catherine Greene's eyes sparkled. "Why, thank you, Eli. That's a real compliment—coming from a New Englander. Tell me about the peddler."

Eli forgot he couldn't talk to a woman. He told her about Hiram Wedge, and how he had died at Bunker Hill, with a broken musket. "He kept his promise to me—about Paul Revere. I hope I keep my promise to him, and amount to something."

"You will make your mark, Eli. It's written in every line of your face."

Eli shook his head. "I'm getting started mighty late. That's why I must go on, I can't just stay here, Madame Greene. I must find work."

Catherine Greene bent over her embroidery again. "This beastly frame! Look how it pulls the threads!"

Eli straightened. "May I see it?"

She laughed. "Now, what can a lawyer do to an embroidery tambour? Say some long Latin words over it?"

Eli smiled, too. But he turned the tambour in his powerful hands. "That's one thing I

can do for her," he thought. "I'll make her a better tambour tomorrow."

But it was a week later before he'd made a tambour that pleased him. It took that long to find seasoned wood and decent tools to work with. Many times Eli wished he were back in his father's shop for half a day, or in New Haven. While he was in Yale, he'd known every carpenter and mechanic in town. One crusty old fellow used to growl, "A mighty good carpenter was ruined when you started to college." But he'd let Eli use his tools.

Finally, the tambour was done. That night after supper Eli laid it in Catherine Greene's lap. He had intended to make a nice little speech of thanks. Instead, he blurted out, "You might try this."

She said, "Oh, dear! I've put you to so much trouble! Just because I fussed about my tambour. You've gone clear to Savannah to find me a better one!"

Eli flushed. "I didn't go to any trouble at all. I made it."

She fitted her embroidery into the new frame. "But it's wonderful! First, you can mend a watch. Now, this! Eli, you're a genius!"

Eli said, "Just a whittling Yankee, a

tinkerer. That's all. When I was twelve, I made a fiddle. When I was fourteen, I had my own business, making nails. I certainly ought to be able to make anything as simple as an embroidery frame."

She stared at him. "A violin when you were twelve? Your own business when you were fourteen? Then why," she asked, "are you studying law?"

"Because there's no future in my mechanical bent. After the war, England dumped cheap goods here and ruined our shops. Most of the young mechanics went west and took up land to farm. My father always said I wasn't worth my salt as a farmer. So I'm studying law."

"I never heard of anything so foolish! Of course there's a future for you in your mechanical bent! You're a genius! There's always a job for genius! All we have to do is to find the right thing."

Eli stood. "Then I'll leave you to find the job. I'll read law." He started up the wide, curving stairway, smiling. "I'll remember this night," he told himself. "It's the first time Eli Whitney ever got the last word with a woman."

He was halfway up the stairs when she

called him. "Eli Whitney, come back here!"

"Yes, Madame Greene?"

She didn't answer. She pulled the bell-cord and rang for Zeb. When the old Negro appeared, she said, "Zeb, find Mr. Phineas. Tell him it's very important."

"Yes, ma'am!" Zeb ducked his white head.

Catherine Greene smiled at Eli. "Sit down. It makes my neck ache to look up at you."

"What it it?" Eli asked.

"We'll wait till Phineas comes," Catherine Greene said mysteriously. "I know the very thing for you to do. But there's no use saying everything twice, is there?"

"Does it have something to do with my mechanical bent?"

"Of course," Catherine answered.

Eli shook his head. "There's no future in that."

Catherine Greene said, "Yes, there is Eli. There's a great need. You are the man who can answer it."

The words sent a shiver down Eli's spine. He looked at Catherine Greene. What was she thinking of? Had his moment come? Would he be like Patrick Henry? Yesterday a nobody, tomorrow a great man? *A great need* . . .

Catherine glanced up from her embroidery. "Eli, do you remember the other day when Major Brewer and his friends were here from Augusta?"

Did he remember! He had never been so bored! Just thinking about it made him want to yawn. But he managed to smile, instead. "The men who'd fought under General Greene? Of course I remember."

She smiled, too. "Poor Eli. You were so disappointed, weren't you?"

Eli turned red. "Whatever makes you say that?"

"Of course you were disappointed." The

general's widow shook her head. "You knew they were officers who'd fought under Nathanael. You thought you'd hear them discuss the battles of the Revolution. You forgot, Eli, that we don't have soldiers in these United States. We just have citizens who fight when they have to. If war comes, they lay down their plows and pick up their guns. When war ends, they lay down their guns and pick up their plows again."

Eli remembered Hiram Wedge and his peddler's wagon. Hiram had left it in Virginia, and come north to fight. Eli remembered all the men of Westborough who'd gone out to fight and then come home to get in the hay. "I never thought of it that way. But I guess it's true. You . . . You . . . certainly can think—for a woman."

She smiled at the compliment. "Oh, it isn't my idea. I heard Nathanael say it a hundred times. Poor Nathanael! He even had to wage war with soldiers who'd lay down their guns in the middle of a campaign. They had to get their crops in." She shook her head. "No soldiers—just citizens. That's why you didn't hear them discuss campaigns the other night. That's why you heard them talk about . . ."

She cocked her head. "By the way, just what did you hear?"

Eli was glad that Phineas came in just then. He didn't have to answer. The truth was he hadn't listened to the talk that flowed around him. He'd been thinking of other things.

Phineas teased Catherine. "Zeb tells me something is very important. Plans for another dance?"

Catherine said, "Phineas, what if I told you there is a machine that will clean the seed from upland cotton?"

Phineas gave a short laugh that sounded more like a bark. He slouched in a chair. "I'd say you're very charming and a little mad."

"Why?"

Phineas explained, as to a child. "My dear Catherine! Men have been growing this green-seed upland cotton for two thousand years. And for most of that time they've been trying to find a quick way to seed it. If there were a machine that would do it, don't you think I'd know about it?"

Catherine said, "If I told you there is going to be such a machine, would you want to put money it it?"

Phineas wasn't slouching now. "I'd invest

every penny I have in the world in it!" he said. "Every penny I could lay my hands on!"

She smiled. "There you are, Eli. A future for your mechanical bent. You shall invent an engine to take the seed out of cotton bolls. Phineas will supply the money you need to develop it. You'll both be rich men."

Phineas slid down in his chair again. He lifted his eyebrows. "What makes you think Eli can do it?" he asked.

"He's a mechanical genius. He's been hiding his light under a bushel—of law books." She laid aside her embroidery. "I wonder where we can find some cotton bolls? Does anyone around here bother to grow cotton?"

Eli was puzzled. "I thought cotton was an important crop?"

She said, "Not yet. It takes too long to free the cotton from seeds. A man can't seed more than a pound a day. But it will be important when there's an engine to seed it."

Eli looked blank.

Phineas jumped to his feet. "Where were you the other night? When those planters talked for three solid hours about upland cotton?"

Catherine said, "He was woolgathering." She explained, "Eli, there are thousands of acres in Georgia and the Carolinas where men could grow upland cotton. With the new machinery in England for spinning, the world is hungry for more cotton."

Eli looked up in surprise. He had heard with a good deal of interest of the machines built by Hargreaves and Arkwright. But it had not occurred to him that the work of these English inventors would have an effect halfway across the world.

Catherine said, "What Hargreaves and Arkwright did was great; what you'll do will be greater."

"Mobs wrecked their homes," Eli said. "Destroyed their machines."

Phineas shrugged. "But that was because their machines took the place of human hands. They put people out of work. A machine to seed upland cotton wouldn't do that. It would give more people a chance to work. As it is now, we can't afford to raise upland cotton because we can't afford to seed it by hand."

Catherine said, "There's a great need, Eli. A great need."

Phineas studied Eli with narrowed eyes. "You really think he can do it? Invent such a machine?"

Catherine said, "I know he can."

Eli got up. "I'm sorry. This is all a waste of time. I'm no inventor. I'm a lawyer. That is—I will be—if I get back to my books."

Phineas challenged. "You can't turn your back on a chance to earn a fortune!"

"Remember what you said?" Eli reminded him. "People have been trying for two thousand years to invent a way to seed that cotton?"

"Exactly!" Phineas argued. "That's why there are millions in your invention!"

Eli looked at the two earnest faces in bewilderment. "You seem to forget that I haven't invented it yet."

"But you can!" Phineas shouted. "If Catherine Greene says you're a genius, you are, whether you want to be or not!"

Catherine soothed him. "Phineas! For goodness' sake!" She looked up at Eli. "A machine to seed upland cotton would make a great difference to our country, Eli."

Eli felt the tingle up his spine again. Yesterday a nobody—tomorrow a great man. Was this his chance? But what about his father's wish that his son become a lawyer? He owed a debt to his father. How long could he afford to forget his law? At last he said, "I'll make a bargain with you."

"Yes, Eli?" Catherine said quietly.

"I'll work on the idea one month. Then . . ."

Phineas started to shout again, but Catherine silenced him. "Yes, Eli?"

"Then, if I don't have any idea what to do, I'll stop and go back to my studies. Agreed?"

Catherine smiled. "It's agreed. If you give up, I won't nag you to go on. And I won't let Phineas nag you, either. But I don't think you'll give up, Eli. Once you start, you'll keep on."

Phineas said, "A month! But, look here—"

Catherine interrupted him. "The next thing to think about is a place for Eli to work on his invention."

Phineas stopped arguing and began to plan. "That's right. A place where our secret will be safe. There's that two-room barn. We can fix it so it will be safe. Bars for the windows. Padlocks on the doors. No one must see the machine till Eli has patented it."

Catherine was puzzled. "Patented it?"

Phineas and Eli told her about the patent law. Under this law, the inventor explains the secret of his invention to the government. If the idea is a new one, the government grants the inventor the exclusive right to his invention for a certain number of years. He alone can make, use, or sell his invention. No other person can copy the idea without paying the inventor for the privilege.

"Patents are granted for new and useful inventions," Phineas said. "A machine to seed upland cotton will certainly be new! And it will certainly be useful. Eli won't have any trouble getting a patent on his invention."

Eli laughed. "After I've invented it? Or before?"

But Phineas didn't hear. He was walking up and down like a caged lion. "We'll manufacture the machine ourselves. And we'll buy up all the cotton and clear it of seed ourelves. That's where the money will be."

Eli said, "Have you any idea how much money it takes to build machinery?"

Phineas shrugged. "Don't worry. After the first season, we'll have our profits to reinvest on machinery. The government patent will protect our exclusive rights. The first thing is a safe place to work."

A week later, the sturdy barn had iron bars at the windows, and a heavy padlock on the door.

The Tired Woman

⫷ A MONTH PASSED. THEN TWO
months. Night after night a light burned late
in the barn. Winter passed. Spring came.
Still the light burned late behind the barred
windows.

No one saw what was in the cabin. But
the whisper began to spread. There was
magic. A fifty-pound bag of upland cotton
would disappear into the barn. In no time at
all, the cotton came out again, seeded.

The whisper crept up the lazy Savannah
River and spread across the pine barrens. The
story grew. Someone knew someone who knew
someone who had seen five hundred pounds of

cotton disappear into the barn at Mulberry Grove where that whittling Yankee worked. Five hundred pounds! In no time at all, it was seeded.

One March night, just after dusk, a large rowboat drifted down the tawny, mud-colored river and nosed into shore near Mulberry Grove. In a moment it was hidden by overhanging trees.

The thin man in the stern moved.

The heavy man at the oars muttered, "No, Cade, we'll wait till midnight."

Cade shrugged his thin shoulders. "We'd better look around and get the lay of the land, Hank."

The oarsman's laugh rumbled in his thick neck. "I don't need to look around. I know where he's working. They've put iron bars on the windows. But we'll get the machine, all right."

Cade's pale blue, close-set eyes narrowed. "I still think my plan is better."

Hank snarled. "Craziest idea I ever heard of. If we want that cotton gin, we've got to break in and take it. And do it before someone else does."

Cade's thin lips curled. "Yes, take it. So Whitney will know it's been stolen. So he'll raise an alarm from here to the governor's house in Savannah. If we follow my plan—"

Hank slouched in the boat. "I said *no*. That's the end of it."

Cade shrugged. Sullenly, he waited for midnight.

At last Hank stirred. "Let's go."

Without a sound the two men crawled from the boat, and shuffled through the trees toward the cabin with barred windows. Hank stopped in disgust. A flicker of candlelight still glinted against the bars. "The fool's still working. We'll have to wait till he stops for the night."

The hours crawled. Dawn began to pale the sky. The candle still flickered.

Cade's mouth twisted. "Think maybe my plan is better?"

Hank snarled, "No!" He led the way back to the boat.

Cade said, "I tell you, I can walk right in there in broad daylight, and see that machine. I can—"

Hank growled, "We'll come back tomorrow night. He can't work that way two nights in a row."

Again, at dusk, the next night, the boat nosed into the hiding place; again the men

snarled at each other and waited for midnight.
Again they crawled from the boat and slipped
through the trees.

When they came in sight of the barred
windows, Hank stopped short.

Cade sneered. "So he can't work that way
two nights in a row?"

Sullenly, Hank led the way back to the boat.
Cade's soft voice jeered. "So now what? Do
I try my plan?"

Hank barked, "All right, try it! It'll serve
you right if he catches on and has you arrested
and put in prison."

Cade laughed softly. "He won't catch on. I could fool my own mother if I tried to. Oh, no! He won't catch on! When that poor old upcountry woman comes to see Mr. Whitney, he won't catch on to a thing."

Hank shoved out from shore and leaned to the oars. His heavy body swung back. The boat leaped.

Cade sat in the stern and laughed.

Inside the barn, Eli rubbed his hand over his aching forehead and stared at the engine he'd made. So near, yet so far. It worked, yes. It seeded cotton. But it should work better. Every time lint clogged the teeth, he had to stop and clean them. How could he get that beastly cotton lint off the cylinder?

Perhaps if he sketched the whole thing, he'd get an idea. He shoved cotton out of his way and spread paper on his workbench. He sharpened a quill pen and began to draw.

His candle guttered in a puddle of wax. Without looking up from his work, Eli reached for another candle, and lighted it. He held it a moment in the candlestick until its chill had hardened the hot wax. He took up his quill again and began to sketch a cross section of the cotton engine.

The second candle burned down, guttered,

and went out. Eli didn't notice. He slept,
slumped forward, his head on his arms, across
the plan for the cotton engine.

Zeb came with breakfast on a tray about
ten the next morning. He hammered on the
door. "Mister Whitney!" No answer. Zeb
shook his head and took the tray back.

About noon, a tall woman with close-set,
pale eyes plodded through the gnarled live
oaks and stopped in sight of the barred windows. She appeared to have come from up
country. Red clay muddied her heavy shoes
and stained the hem of her coarse homespun
skirt. She must have come a long way. She
sagged against a tree, as though too tired to
take another step.

An hour passed; two hours. The woman
never stirred.

In the middle of the afternoon, old Zeb
came toward the barn again with another tray.
The tall woman straightened. Her pale eyes
narrowed.

Zeb called at the barn door. Eli opened it.
"Yes, Zeb? Breakfast?"

Zeb chuckled. "Breakfast? This is dinner.
It's most nigh three o'clock. Mister Whitney,
if this was judgment day, it'd take two angels
to stir you." Still chuckling, he gave Eli the

tray. He turned. He stopped. He caught his breath sharply. "You there, under that tree? What you hangin' around here for?"

The tired woman plodded forward, her pale gaze fixed on Eli. "Mr. Whitney, sir, I've come a far piece to Mulberry Grove, to see you. I been waiting all morning."

Eli said, "It's all right, Zeb. We don't have to worry about women."

Zeb moved off, muttering to himself.

Eli balanced the tray on one hand and held open the door. "You're hungry, aren't you? Come in and sit down."

The country woman entered the workshop. She slumped on a chair, her elbows on her spread knees, her gnarled hands dangling. Everything about her sagged. Everything but her pale eyes! Her eyes darted about the shop and came to rest on a box with the crank on the side.

Eli divided the food on two plates: roast chicken, rosy slices of ham, sweet potatoes, hot biscuits, and little fruit pies.

The woman stood. Her pale eyes studied the drawings that lay by the cotton engine. When Eli looked up from the tray, she went quickly to his side. She picked up a fork from the tray, turned it in her hands, and frowned, shaking her head.

Eli said, "They call it a fork. We didn't have many where I came from. Just knives and spoons. Would you like to try it?"

She shook her head, and laid the fork down. She took the plate he handed her and sat again. She wolfed her food with her fingers and wiped her hands on her skirt.

When they had finished eating, Eli said, "You feel better now?" His curious visitor nodded. "Why did you want to see me?"

For a moment she was silent, as though hunting for words. "Mr. Whitney, up country, in the pine barrens, where I come from, we're kind of shut away."

Eli nodded. "I know how that is."

"All my life, I've wanted to see someone great, just once," the woman blurted. "I could tell my children and my grandchildren."

Eli Whitney flushed. "You don't mean that's why you wanted to see me?"

The hoarse, tired voice talked on. "I remember, six—seven years ago, a stranger came up our way. He told us how General Greene, him that saved Georgia from the British, was a-living here at Mulberry Grove. I said to myself, 'Sara, you get along down there to Mulberry Grove and see him.' " Her eyes begged Eli to understand. "I did want to see someone great just once. We're kind of shut away."

Eli nodded. "I know. You feel you never hear about anything till it's over and done with."

The woman brought the empty plate to Eli and stood by the workbench. Her gaze drifted to the drawing.

The tired voice drawled on. "I was bound and determined to see the general. But seemed like there never was a chance to get away. Always the plowing, the planting, the chopping, the hoeing. Always the spinning, the weaving, the butchering. Always the soap-making. Every time I was ready to up and go, something would happen. Or one of the young ones would sicken."

"You didn't get to come?" Eli was touched by the country woman's tale.

"I came." The visitor leaned closer over Eli's shoulder. "But it was too late. I didn't know till I got here, how the general had died of a sunstroke. Dead and buried, he was, three months back, when I got here."

"He didn't get to enjoy Mulberry Grove very long," Eli said.

The woman nodded blankly. "I came a fair piece, and it was too late. Then, just a while back, I heard the President was a-coming to see us. I heard he would be at Mulberry Grove."

Eli said, "That's right. He visited here."

"I was bound and determined I'd see him," she said. "I came again. But I was too late. He'd been and gone in these parts. He'd started up river to Augusta. I followed along for a bit. I thought he might stop somewhere a spell, and I'd see him."

Her tired gaze was still fixed on the drawings. "Everywhere I went, people told how they'd seen him. Four, five people I talked to. One man told me how a crowd gathered by the road. The President got out of his stagecoach and mounted his horse, so a body could see him. He rode, fine and tall, on his horse, and lifted his hat. It was almost like seeing him, to hear about it."

"But you didn't get to see him?"

The woman shook her bowed head. "No. That's why I've come again. I figure this is my last chance to see somebody great, or to see something wonderful." She stared at the box, the cotton engine.

Eli flushed and smiled. "You're not classing me with generals and presidents?"

The woman put out a bony hand and smoothed the wooden box of the cotton engine. "Yes, Mr. Whitney. I'm putting you right up there with them both. General Greene saved Georgia from the British. The President — when he was a fighting man—he saved the whole country. But you're going to do something just as great. You're going to save us from starving."

Eli said, "Hardly that."

"You and your cotton gin they tell about." She shortened the word engine to 'gin. Her bony hand smoothed the box again. "You don't know what it's like, up country. That land of ours is no count for anything. It'll grow this green-seed cotton. That's about all. But what's the use of growing it? We work from can-see to can't-see, tending it. Then what we got? Them pesky seeds. Takes a body a whole day to seed a pound."

Eli said, "I can believe that."

The tired voice took on a soothing tone. "Now we hear tell about a cotton gin. We're hoping. We're hoping we can raise a money crop on our worthless land." The woman looked at Eli. "That's why I wanted to tell my children and grandchildren I saw you. I tells 'em I came a far piece and talked to Mr. Whitney. How he let me see the cotton gin when it was a-borning!"

Eli hesitated.

She said, "Of course, I won't understand nothing. I know that. But I can tell 'em I saw it when it was a-borning."

Eli shrugged and smiled. "All right. You may look at it."

She lifted the lid on the box. She stared in it, shaking her head. She turned the crank. She sighed and closed the lid again. "It's all beyond me. But I can tell them I saw it. Some day, when you're famous, I'll be able to say I saw Mr. Whitney." She plodded to the door. "Thank you kindly, sir."

The tired woman shuffled slowly along until she was out of sight of the barred windows. Then she picked up her skirts and ran. She slid down the bank to the waiting boat.

"Get caught?" Hank asked.

Cade laughed, and pulled off the skirt. "Of course not. I told you I wouldn't."

Hank jeered, "Then you didn't get in."

Cade's thin mouth twisted. "Oh, yes, I did. Of all the luck! His drawings were spread right on the workbench. Plain as the nose on your face. I didn't even have to see in the gin to know how it works. But I did see inside the little box. Just to prove I could."

Hank said, "All right, all right. Can you describe it?"

Cade lifted his eyebrows. "I can make it. Of all simple things—once you get the idea. I told you my plan was best, didn't I?"

Hank dropped his sneering tone. "All right," he said. "So what's it like?"

Cade lifted his eyebrows again. "You mean, I tell you?"

Hank reddened. "Aren't we in this together?"

Cade's lips twisted. "Not on a fifty-fifty split. After all, I'm the one who got the plan. Let's say one-third for you, and two-thirds for me."

Hank pounded his fist on his knee and swore. Cade watched him with pale, narrowed eyes and laughed.

Savannah Fever

◗ IN SAVANNAH, MR. CHANDLER, a commission merchant, studied the accounts of the planters he dealt with. All year Mr. Chandler let the planters have things on credit. Every ship that arrived in Savannah brought goods for the planters: machinery, furniture, clothes, carriages. Mr. Chandler paid for everything. Then, when the planters harvested their crops, they settled their accounts with him.

Some planters always had money ahead in Mr. Chandler's records. Some planters were always in debt, depending on next year's profits. Some planters were two years behind in their accounts — or even three. Mr. Chandler shook his head over one record. He wrote a note and addressed it to one John Morrow, of Pine Acres.

An obliging traveler carried the letter for Mr. Chandler. The Morrow plantation was four days up river from Savannah to Augusta, and another day from Augusta to Pine Acres.

John Morrow's young wife watched her husband read the note. "What is it, John? Something wrong?"

John managed to smile. "No, no, Lucinda. Just a little matter of business." He crossed the wide veranda that shaded the big house of the plantation. He leaned against one of the tall white pillars and stared off down the long tree-shaded drive. "I'm going to have to make a trip to Savannah."

"Oh, John! Not clear to Savannah! You'll be at least ten days just going and coming back!"

John continued to stare down the drive. "I'll be well taken care of. I'm—I'm going to take Old Ephriam's boys with me."

"All three of them? Young Eph, and the twins?"

"All three." John Morrow's voice was tense and hard.

Lucinda was puzzled. "But won't they be missed? I've heard you say they're the best field hands you have."

John turned and sat down, his elbows on his knees, his head in his hands. "No, they won't be missed," he muttered. "There isn't enough work here to keep fifty slaves busy. Twenty, maybe, or twenty-five, but not fifty."

Lucinda said, "John, what is wrong? You've got to tell me!"

He got up restlessly. "Let's walk around, shall we?"

At dusk, they paused near the row of cabins where the Negro field hands lived. They watched the wood smoke curl from the chimneys, heard the music of a banjo, the rich, throaty sound of laughter.

John shook his head slowly. "Fifty people to clothe and feed. Fifty people to care for when they're sick. To try to find work for when they're well. Lucinda, what else can I do?"

Mrs. Morrow walked on for a few rods in silence. Then she said, "I don't understand."

"We're poor, Lucinda. Land poor and

slave poor. Slavery is a mistake, Lucinda, in this part of the country. On the rice plantations the planters can come out ahead. But I can't. Pine Acres can't support fifty slaves."

Lucinda's face whitened. "John, you're not going to sell Ephriam's boys?"

Her husband didn't answer.

"But you can't do that, John," Lucinda begged. "Those boys were born here. You'd break Old Ephriam's heart! And Maria's, too. She and Young Eph want to get married."

"I've got to raise money, Lucinda."

"Then sell part of our land," she said, staring through the trees to the shadowy fields, the wide acres beyond.

John looked at her wearily. "Who'd want it?"

The next morning when he said good-by, he looked troubled. "Lucinda, I . . ." He stopped. "I'll be back in two weeks." He kissed her, and swung into his saddle.

Young Eph and the twins, Cato and Lycurgus, followed in the wagon, drawn by four mules.

Maria came to the gate, calling after young Eph. "Don't you forget me while you're off seeing the city."

Young Eph laughed and cracked his whip high over the four mules.

Old Eph beamed. "Sure is nice of Mister John to take my boys clear to Savannah."

Lucinda Morrow flushed and ran into the great house.

The day they expected John Morrow back, Old Eph scolded Lucinda gently. "You ain't eatin', Miss Lucinda. Mister John won't like it when he gets back. Yes, ma'am. He depends on Old Eph. On Old Eph and his boys."

Lucinda laid down her fork. "I—I—don't want to be disturbed, Eph. I'll be in my room." She fled.

John Morrow got back at sunset. He raced up the stairs. "Lucinda! Where are you?"

Lucinda said, "John! You're smiling"

He laughed. "Our troubles are over! Come —look out the window!"

She looked. Their wagon was going toward the barns. The twins were in it. "Where's Young Eph?"

A second wagon followed the first, drawn by five new mules. Young Eph drove.

"John, you didn't sell Eph's boys!" Mrs. Morrow's sorrow was banished. "But how could you afford . . ."

John said, "Oh, I borrowed some money. But don't worry. This fall, when we sell our crop, I'll pay back everything I owe."

"But what can we raise? You've said this land is good for nothing but green-seed cotton."

John beamed. "That's it, my dear!"

Lucinda's eyes widened with fright. "John, are you sick?"

"I never felt better! And now, not another word till after supper."

When they'd eaten, and Eph served coffee, John lifted his cup. "Lucinda, let's drink a toast to a man I've never seen, and a man you've never heard of. *To Eli Whitney!*"

Lucinda repeated the toast. *"To Eli Whitney!* But who," she asked, "is Eli Whitney?"

John only smiled. "Did you notice I had five new mules? They're for plowing."

His wife hestitated. "John, you didn't mean that about planting upland cotton, did you?"

"Indeed, I did! Acres of it!" John's eyes glinted.

"But it's late to plant more. It's the middle of April."

John explained. "I've a month yet that I can plant. The middle of May isn't too late. Even the first of June. It's a bit risky, that late.

But it's worth the risk. Believe me, it's worth the risk"

Lucinda said, "But John, how will you seed it?"

John beamed. "With Eli Whitney's cotton gin! He's invented a gin to seed the upland cotton. Just as easily as the roller-gins seed the sea-island cotton. Lucinda, our troubles are over!"

Mrs. Morrow sighed with relief. "I was afraid you'd caught the fever in Savannah."

John laughed. "Maybe I have! Savannah fever! But it's a new kind of fever! The cotton fever! I tell you the whole town was talking upland cotton!"

A shadow of worry crossed Lucinda's face. "You are more deeply in debt than ever, aren't you?"

John shrugged. "Until I sell my crop this fall."

"If . . . if . . . anything happened, and you didn't get the cotton gin . . ." Lucinda's voice sank to an anxious whisper.

John's hands clenched the edge of the table. His knuckles whitened. "Don't say that, Lucinda. Don't ever think such a thing! If I couldn't seed the crop I'm going to plant. . . . Don't ever say such a thing!"

And Another Fever

⊂ӟ ELI REALIZED SOMEONE HAD been knocking on the barn door a long time. "Coming!" He went to the door, lifted the heavy bar, and opened it. "Yes, Catherine? Supper time?"

Catherine entered the shop. "It was suppertime hours ago. It's past midnight. You haven't had a decent night's sleep in weeks. What in the world is wrong?"

Eli scowled. "That pesky engine."

"But you've done what nobody else has ever done. You've seeded green-seed cotton by machinery."

Eli continued to scowl. "It doesn't work as well as it should."

Catherine said, "Tell me about it."

Eli grinned wearily. "What does a woman know about machinery?"

She smiled. "Nothing. But it might help you to talk about it."

Eli shrugged and opened the top of the box. "You see that curved partition with openings in it? Now watch." Eli turned the crank. Little curved wires reached through the slits.

Catherine nodded.

Eli heaped the top compartment with cotton bolls and closed the box. He turned the crank. He opened it again. "Now, look."

Where the heap of cotton had been there was nothing but seeds.

"You see," the inventor said, "the wire teeth seize the cotton and pull it through the slits. The seeds are too big to go through the slits. Only the clean lint goes through. The seeds are left behind."

Catherine Greene looked into the second compartment, which was full of clean, seedless cotton lint. "How much cotton can you seed in a day with a machine like this model?" she asked.

"Oh, forty or fifty pounds," Eli answered. "That is—I'll have forty or fifty pounds of lint. That much seed cotton would weigh a hundred and fifty or two hundred pounds. The seeds are far heavier than the lint."

"But, Eli, that's magnificent! I don't see why you're not satisfied."

He said, "Because it should be better." He lifted the curved partition and showed her the cylinder with its rows of wire teeth. Cotton lint clung to them. "I won't stop tinkering until I find a way to keep the lint from sticking to the teeth."

Catherine cocked her head to one side. "Then for goodness' sake, let's do something about it."

"Yes. Let's do something. By all means," Eli jeered.

Catherine went to the fireplace and brought a brush. "I'll hold this brush against the teeth. Now you turn the crank, while I hold the brush."

Eli shouted, "Do you know what you've done, Catherine?"

She jumped back in confusion. "Oh, dear, did I break something?"

Eli didn't answer. He made elbow room on the cluttered workbench, spread paper, and sharpened a quill. "Brushes! I'll add a second cylinder with brushes! To turn in the opposite direction." He began to draw.

Catherine flushed. "Did I ruin your model?"

Eli laughed. "No! You solved my last problem!"

She said, "Oh, about the brush? But that was perfectly simple. You'd have thought of it sooner or later."

Eli said, "The whole machine is perfectly simple—after someone thinks of it."

She said, "Eli Whitney! You aren't going to work any longer tonight, are you?"

Eli didn't answer. He didn't even realize she had gone until she came back with Phineas.

Phineas looked at the sketch as Eli explained it. He shouted, "Eli, you've done it! Catherine said you were a genius! Now the thing is to get the patent, and get to making the engines immediately! Where do you think the factory should be located? In Augusta, perhaps? It's closer to the region where they'll grow upland cotton."

Eli said. "No. In New Haven."

Phineas stared. "New Haven? But here's where we'll use the machines!"

"Not till they're built. I need good tools, good material, and skilled workmen."

Phineas nodded slowly. "I see what you mean."

"I can build the machines in New Haven, and ship them to Savannah, faster than I can build them down here."

Phineas frowned a moment, and finally nodded. "Maybe that's better. We're certainly going to need all the machines we can get by fall."

Eli said, "I'll write to Charles Horner, in New Haven. He's a fine mechanic. I'll tell him to try to get a building for me. There's one on Wooster Street. And I'll need at least two dozen workmen."

Phineas said, "Fine! Come on! We'll celebrate."

"You celebrate," Eli said. "I'm going to write to Charles Horner. And then I'm going to start building a new machine."

Phineas stared. "But why?"

"Because my application for a patent must describe the machine exactly; everything about it. I must try out the idea of brushes, and be sure they'll work. And I must describe them in my application for a patent."

When Eli's improved model of his machine

was done, he made his drawings and mailed a package to Thomas Jefferson, Secretary of State, at the capital in Philadelphia. It was his application for a patent on his new and useful invention, the cotton engine.

"Or, as they call it down here," Eli thought, "the 'cotton gin.' I suppose, some day, no one will know what the machine was called in the first place."

Three days later, Eli started out to drive north in a two-wheeled chaise. Everywhere that he stopped overnight, he listened hungrily to the talk of other travelers. It seemed to him that for months he had been shut away from the world, buried in the work on his invention.

Everywhere, people were talking about France, and the French Republic's war with England. Some people thought the United States should side with France because she was a republic, because she had come to the help of the Americans in the Revolution. Other men were pleased that President Washington had declared we would keep out of Europe's quarrels.

Eli remembered what Catherine Greene had said about our citizen army; that we didn't really have soldiers—only citizens who took up arms when needed. He didn't see, if that was true now, how we could be much help to France, even if Washington had wanted to side with the Republic.

Listening to the hot words along the road and in the inns, Eli realized he couldn't solve the country's problem. His problem was to manufacture his cotton engine. His problem was to get to New Haven as soon as possible. With luck, he might make the trip from Savannah to New Haven in three weeks. . . .

A month later, he was on the Lower Post Road, nearing New Haven. "I'll write to Phineas and Catherine tonight," he thought, "and tell them about the trip." When he sat down to write, however, he felt that there was no use telling them about the mud hole that swallowed his horse belly-deep and broke both wheels of his chaise. There was no use telling them he'd lost his books when a ferry upset. There was, he decided, no use in worrying them.

"I wish I could tell them about the Conestoga wagons—what it meant to see them," Eli thought.

But what could he say? Just that he'd been stopped at a crossroad one day, while thirty Conestoga wagons crowded the road, going west. Just that they were the freight carriers of the new country opening farther and farther west. Just that they were built like boats on wheels, the bodies swooping high, back and front, to keep freight from sliding on hills. Just that the bodies were red and blue, and the canvas cover was white.

What else could he say? How could he make them understand what it meant to see red, white and blue moving west with a growing country? His country!

How could he picture the wagoners who drove the Conestoga wagons? Tough and confident. So proud, they seemed to swagger, sitting still. How could he explain that these wagoners all had the look of Hiram Wedge?

Eli shook his head. It wouldn't be any use to try. He'd just say the trip was uneventful.

Suddenly, he saw the red cliffs that loomed above Mill River. New Haven! He leaned forward and slapped the reins.

He'd drive straight to Charles Horner's house. They'd invite him to supper. Baked beans and brown bread. He'd ride the twins on his shoulder. He'd shake hands with Tim. Tim was fourteen. Eli remembered what it was like to be fourteen. He remembered how it felt to want to fill a man's place in the world.

Eli turned into the lane he called *Horner Street* because Horners' house was the only building on it. A man yelled, and ran from across the road.

"Stop! Don't go any closer!"

"What's wrong?" Eli hesitated, dangling the reins.

"The black vomit," the stranger shouted.

The black vomit . . . yellow fever! Eli shuddered.

The man said, "They all died. All but the boy."

"Where's he? Where's Tim?" Eli Whitney shouted.

"Over at Andrew's Tavern. He was away when they all came down with it. All over before he got home. Lucky for him."

Lucky. . . . Eli remembered when his own mother had died. Tim Horner had lost all his family. His kind, slow-spoken father, his mother, his little sisters.

Slowly Eli drove to Andrew's Tavern. Tim Horner was there, helping the stable boys. Tall for his age, Tim had looked like his mother, rosy-cheeked and merry. But now he was haggard.

Tim saw Eli and came to him. "Father

didn't get your letter, Mr. Whitney. Mr. Andrew gave it to me. He paid the postage himself, and gave it to me. He's mighty obliging, isn't he? I've done what I could. You can get the building on Wooster Street. But it'll be a little hard about the workmen. Three of them you wanted, they—they— went like my people."

Eli thought, "If I say the wrong thing, he'll cry." He said, "Thank you, Tim, for taking charge. Would you like to work for me?"

Tim hesitated. "I don't know much about tools."

"No one knows anything about what I'm going to be doing. We'll all learn together." Eli spoke quietly.

Tim steadied. "I'd like that. I'd like that fine. Mr. Whitney, did they—did they tell you how the yellow fever started? A fellow opened a trunk from the West Indies. He came down first. Then I guess people caught it from him and other people from them, and. . ." Tim slapped a mosquito. "You know what Mr. Andrew says? He says he doesn't know which has been worse this summer—yellow fever or mosquitoes." He laughed shakily, and clenched and unclenched his hands.

Eli said, "I'll go talk to Mr. Andrew right now about your working for me. Then we'll go look at the building on Wooster Street. We're going to be the two busiest men in New Haven."

Tim straightened. "Yes, sir."

Mr. Andrew agreed that it would be a fine thing for the boy to work with Mr. Whitney —a privilege he called it. Eli asked about the letter from the capital in Philadelphia. Mr. Andrew shook his head. "Nothing's come, Mr. Whitney. I'll let you know the minute it does."

That night, in spite of his aching tiredness, Eli was slow going to sleep. Problems buzzed in his brain, thick as the mosquitoes in New Haven. Workmen must be found, in spite of yellow fever. There'd be supplies to get, machines to build. And it had to be done in a hurry, too. It was already past the middle of June.

A good thing it was summer. Men always worked from dawn to dusk. Their work day was only about ten hours in the winter. But in the summer they could get in a good fourteen or sixteen hours.

About one thing Eli was confident. He'd have the patent in plenty of time. Travel was much faster in the north than in the south. The stagecoach made the trip from Philadelphia to New York now in less than two days, and post riders were even faster.

"Yes, I'll be hearing from Philadelphia just any day," Eli told himself.

June wore into July. August came, and still there was no word from Philadelphia. In the Wooster Street shop, the men worked from "can-see to can't-see." Eli stretched his day from before dawn to midnight.

It was an hour yet till dawn, one late August morning, when he sat in the Wooster Street shop, writing to Phineas by candlelight.

. . . No word from Philadelphia. It must be because of the yellow fever. It's been bad enough here, but much worse in the capital. People are dying by hundreds. Half the city is trying to escape to the country. The country people are trying to drive them back, for fear they'll bring the sickness with them. . . .

Tim opened the door. "There's a letter for you at the tavern, Mr. Whitney."

Eli jumped up. "From Philadelphia?"

"No, sir. From Mr. Miller. Want me to get it for you?"

Eli slumped to the bench again. "No hurry. I can guess what it says, and there's nothing I can do about it."

He laid aside the letter he was writing, and picked up an iron fitting for one of his machines. No matter how carefully the men worked, Eli always checked a part before it was heated and hardened. He checked, shook his head, and picked up a file.

Tim said, "Shall I get the forge going?"

"No hurry, Tim. This is going to take time."

Tim watched in silence. After a while, he said, "Before you can heat and temper that, you have to file and measure and file and measure, don't you?"

Eli nodded. "Until it's exact."

"And then you start on another piece. File and measure; file and measure." Tim shook his head. "Making things exact certainly is a slow business."

"Yes," Eli said. "Some day, when I have time to think, I'll figure a way around this."

Sunrise came, and the workmen plodded in. Eli answered their questions. When they were all settled at work, Eli went to the tavern with Tim for breakfast.

Mr. Andrew gave him the letter from Phineas. "Just one page, this time," he said.

Eli paid the quarter for postage on one page.

Tim looked at the letter. "I wonder what he says this time?"

"Just the same thing, probably. That we must have the machines in Georgia by September at the latest. And all I can write back is that the patent hasn't come yet."

He explained to Tim about the patent. A patent, he said, was a statement from the government saying that no one else could copy his invention without his permission. If it weren't for the patent, anyone who saw the machine could copy it. That was why he couldn't ship any of the machines from the Wooster Street shop until he had the patent.

"No matter what Phineas Miller says, I can't ship the machines yet," Eli said.

He opened the letter, and caught his breath as he stared at the page. Just six lines. Someone had broken into the barn and had stolen the cotton engine. If their machines weren't ready by fall, there would be imitations of Eli's cotton engine all over the state!

Tim called, "Hey! Come back! You haven't had your breakfast, Mr. Whitney!"

Eli shook his head and kept walking.

The Bargain

⊂⋿ AT PINE ACRES, JOHN MORROW'S cotton had bloomed. Millions of creamy white blossoms, opening, turning pink, and falling.

Lucinda Morrow had said, "It's beautiful, John! Beautiful!"

John smiled. "Not as beautiful as it will be when it's cotton, bursting the bolls!"

Lucinda shivered.

John looked at her quickly. "What's wrong?"

"I'm sorry. But the thought of this much

cotton still frightens me. Will you really get your cotton gin, John?"

John laughed at her fear. "Don't worry about that. Mr. Chandler, in Savannah, will see that I get the use of a cotton gin. He's just as interested in this crop as I am. That's where I borrowed the money."

Lucinda said, "Of course. It's silly of me to worry."

"It certainly is. There's nothing to worry about."

But when the long summer drought came, John began to worry. After all, he had planted his cotton very late. Had there been time for that long tap root to go deep into the ground? It took time for roots to go deep enough to find moisture, so the plant could stay alive in a drought.

John grew edgy. At dawn, when the horn called the field hands to work, John would get up, too, and ride to the fields. At ten, he'd come in for breakfast, worn out by the heat.

Lucinda watched his haggard face anxiously. "John, it's too hot for you!" she'd say.

"I know. I shan't go out again." Then he'd pace the floor, restless as a cat, wondering if the men were plowing just right.

Finally, the last plowing was done. The crop was "laid by," waiting for the bolls to burst open.

John said, "Lucinda, we've won! It's a magnificent crop."

Lucinda said, "Have you heard from Mr. Chandler—about the cotton gin?"

John's smile faded. "No. I can't understand it. He knows I must have the gin."

The days crawled by, and the nights. Still no word of the cotton gin.

John finally said, "I'll have to go to Savannah for it."

"John, it's so far! And such a hot trip now!"

He said, "I'll be back in two weeks. I'll have to. They're almost ready to begin picking. I have to get that cotton seeded and baled. If I don't, we'll be smothered in cotton."

John had been gone a week when the stranger came to Pine Acres. Jones, he said his name was, Cade Jones. A thin, wiry man, with close-set, pale blue eyes. He talked to Lucinda.

"I see you're going to have quite a bit of cotton to gin. Got a problem on your hands, haven't you?"

Lucinda said, "Not at all. Everything is ready."

He said, "Yes, I see you have a mighty fine press to bale it. What about the gin?"

Lucinda smiled. "My husband is bringing it from Savannah."

"You sure?" There was a sneer in Cade's tone.

"Of course." Lucinda spoke confidently but her heart was pounding.

Cade's pale eyes narrowed. "What if he doesn't?"

Lucinda didn't answer.

He said, "We might make a deal. Your crop's later than mine. I'll bring my gin over and gin your cotton for you. On shares. Say I get a fourth of the cotton for ginning it."

Lucinda blazed. "You get a fourth of it? After we've had all the work and the worry? It's our land and our cotton!"

The man's thin lips twisted. "A fourth of it—if we make a bargain today. Next week, my rate will go up. You sure you don't want to make a bargain with me?"

"I certainly don't." Lucinda felt as if she would smother.

Cade shrugged his thin shoulders. "No bargain today? Too bad. I'll see you again." He shuffled away.

John Morrow was back in ten days. His eyes were sunken, has face drawn. There was no cotton gin to be had. Something about the delay of the patent.

Lucinda said, "But there are gins! A man was here the other day. A terrible creature." She told John about Cade Jones.

"He's lying, Lucinda. There aren't any gins."

But the next morning, the man was back, in a wagon, drawn by mules. On the wagon was a wooden box, with a crank on the side.

"I thought we might make a little bargain, Mr. Morrow. I see you're ready to gin your cotton. I'm all through. Planted earlier than you did, I guess."

John's eyes brightened. "You really have a cotton gin there?"

"I do." Cade chuckled. It pleased him to remember how he'd got the plans for the gin.

"You can gin this green-seed cotton?"

"I ginned mine," Cade answered, with a shrug.

"But where'd you get the gin?" John blurted out the question. He saw a scowl cross the stranger's face.

"I built it," Cade replied shortly.

"But . . . but . . . where'd you get the idea?"

Cade's mouth twisted. "I ain't saying. You want your cotton ginned?"

"I certainly do." Getting Pine Acres cotton ready to market was more important to John Morrow than the question of how this man had got hold of his machine.

Cade said, "I tried to make a bargain with your wife. But she refused. Too bad. I offered to do it for a fourth of the crop. Now the rate's gone up. It's fifty-fifty now. I get half the crop."

John stiffened. "Half the crop? I'll see you

hanged first! I'm willing to pay you a decent fee for the use of your gin! But that's robbery!"

The man shrugged his thin shoulders. "I'll give you half an hour to make up your mind. Then my rate goes up again."

John stormed. "But after all my work, I get only half my crop!"

Cade smiled. "What'll you get if it isn't ginned? Got a place to store it? Can you afford to hold it? . . . Kind of got you there, haven't I?"

John bit the words out through clenched teeth. "All right. For half the crop."

Cade nodded. "I'll need some mules to run your press. And about half a dozen good hands at the gin, to fetch and carry and turn the crank."

John snapped, "You expect me to furnish the men?"

"Of course. You furnish everything but the gin." He swaggered off to his wagon.

Lucinda said, "John, where do you suppose he got the gin? Is it—honest—for him to have it?"

Her husband refused to discuss that problem. He snapped. "I don't know and I don't care! All I know is my crop has to be ginned!"

The Nightmare

◖ THE NIGHTMARE GRIPPED ELI again. In his dream, an avalanche of cotton rolled down a hill to smother him. He struggled and cried out.

A deep voice said, "You're all right, Mr. Whitney."

Eli opened his eyes, looked into the face of a stranger, and tried to remember where he was. He struggled to sit up.

The man said, "Just lie still, Mr. Whitney. You've been a pretty sick man."

Eli sank back on the pillow and looked at

the man again. "I don't seem to remember you."

"I'm Dr. Garst," the doctor answered quietly.

"Dr. Garst?" Eli could not recall any such name. "You haven't been in New Haven very long, have you?"

"You're not in New Haven, Mr. Whitney. You're in New York City."

New York City! Eli shivered, remembering the long months of the summer of '93 while he waited on the patent. From June to September. No word. October. No word. Finally, in November, a letter from Philadelphia at last!

But it had not been the patent. Just a letter telling him that he must send a model of the machine. As soon as that was received, the patent would be issued immediately.

Eli remembered the frantic haste until the model was on its way to Philadelphia. Then more days of waiting. December . . . January . . . February. In March, the patent was issued. March, 1794. But that was a year ago. The sick man struggled to recall where the year had gone to.

"It's March again," he thought painfully. "March, 1795."

Eli remembered again why he had come to New York. "Dr. Garst, I must get back to my shop. When I'm not there . . ."

Dr. Garst snapped, "Man, do you want to kill yourself?"

Eli said, "No danger of that. I'm strong as an ox."

"That so? When they called me, you were weak as a cat and out of your head."

Eli said, "Just a touch of fever. I got it in Georgia. Something to do with the bad air in swamps. It comes back sometimes. But I'm all right now, and I must get back to New Haven. I promised my workmen I'd be back by the eleventh at the latest."

Dr. Garst said, "The eleventh of what?"

"March, of course! And I have things to see about in New York before I go back. I must—"

"Mr. Whitney," the doctor spoke soothingly. "It is now the fourteenth of March."

"No! It can't be!"

"But it is. I tell you, man, you've been very sick."

Eli said, "The fourteenth! Then I must go immediately."

Dr. Garst exploded impatiently. "Sometimes I have a notion to put a sign on my door: 'No merchants, shipbuilders, inventors, or suchlike rich men will be treated.' "

Suchlike rich men. Eli thought of the unpaid bills, the workmen waiting for their wages.

"You're money mad, the lot of you!" Garst said. "Never satisfied with what you have! Oh no, you all have to make a fortune! You rich men kill yourselves, and the doctor gets the blame."

Eli asked, "What makes you think I'm rich?"

The doctor looked surprised. "Didn't you invent the cotton gin, Mr. Whitney?"

"Yes."

"Well, I know what cotton's been doing." Garst shrugged. "I read a piece just the other day in the *Gazette.* Ten years ago—in 1785 —we had just five bags of this cotton to export to England. And the collector at the port seized it, because they said it couldn't possibly have been produced here. And in '93, the very year you invented the cotton gin, we produced over five million pounds of cotton! Think of it! Five million pounds!"

Eli smiled wryly. "I do think of it. Sometimes I have nightmares about it. You see, they produced five million pounds of cotton before my machine was patented." He told Garst about the long delay.

"From June '93 to March '94? But that's criminal!"

Eli said, "Do you remember the yellow fever epidemic in '93, the way it was in Philadelphia?"

Garst sobered. "I worked in it. It was a horror. Life in the city was completely at a standstill."

Eli said, "Yes. Everything waited on death. Including my patent." He shifted to ease the ache in his bones. "The machine I left at Mulberry Grove, in Georgia, was stolen. So, while I waited on the patent, men built imitations of my machine all over the state."

The doctor glared. "Then get after them! Haul them into court! Sue the criminals! Get out an injunction against them. You know, your patent won't be worth a penny if you don't clean out the pirated machines. No man is going to pay a decent price for ginning cotton on your machine if his neighbor is using a pirated one without paying for it."

Eli nodded wearily. "That's right. And that's what we're doing. Sueing them. But, you know, doctor, court trials and lawyers cost money. More money than we have. So, instead of being 'suchlike rich men,' we're in debt."

The doctor gulped. "You—the inventor of the greatest single invention in America—in debt?"

"In debt." Eli spoke soberly. "I'm building machines, as fast as I can. The men are willing. They work hard. But, when problems come up, I have to be there to solve them. When I came away, we had ten machines almost ready to ship to Georgia. I'll wager they haven't gone yet."

Garst shook his head. "You do have a problem, Mr. Whitney. And I promise you I'll get you on your feet and back there just as soon as possible. In ten days or two weeks at the latest."

"Ten days or two weeks?" Eli tried to shout, but could only speak in a hoarse whisper. "Doctor, every hour I'm gone is threatening us with ruin! I've got to go now!"

Someone knocked on the door. Dr. Garst opened it, and stepped outside. He issued orders for quiet, but not before Eli recognized Tim Horner's voice.

What was Tim doing over here in New

York? When Eli had left the plant, Tim had said, "I'll be right here, Mr. Whitney! Doing everything I can!" And now he was whispering to this strange doctor outside the door.

It seemed to Eli that Tim and the doctor talked forever. Finally the doctor let Tim come in.

The doctor said, "I'm going now, Mr. Whitney. I'll see you tomorrow." He looked at Tim sternly. "Just a few minutes. Don't tire him. And don't worry him."

Tim gulped. "Yes, sir."

Dr. Garst went. Tim sat uneasily on the edge of a chair and studied the ceiling. "We—we —heard you were sick, Mr. Whitney, and we were all upset."

Eli said, "How are things at the shop?"

Tim studied the floor. "Just fine, Mr. Whitney. Everything's fine. Except that we're worried about you. So I thought I'd better come over and tell you how things are *there,* and then go back and tell the men how things are *here,* so—so . . ."

Eli said, "Tim Horner, you couldn't tell a lie if your life depended on it. What's wrong?"

Tim hunched his shoulders and was silent.

Eli said, wryly, "Don't worry about me. Bad news won't kill me. If bad news could kill me, I'd have been dead a long time ago."

Tim wet his lips. "Mr. Whitney, the factory burned. It burned to the ground."

The room began to spin. Eli closed his eyes to steady it. "How much did they get out?"

"Nothing." Tim wiped the moisture off his brow.

Eli didn't want to ask the next question, but he had to. "The ten machines that were just finished?"

"They're ruined. Everything's gone. Everything."

Eli opened his eyes again.

Tim said, "Mr. Whitney, tell me what I can do to help! I'll do anything I can. Anything."

Eli said, "Yes, Tim. I know. Find my clothes, and help me dress."

Tim stared. "But, Mr. Whitney, it's no use! Everything's gone, I tell you!"

Eli said, "Yes, Tim. I heard you. Everything's gone. So I have to start over. And then . . . keep on."

The Nature of Muskets

⊂⧵ WHEN ELI GOT BACK TO NEW Haven, he stared at the blackened ruins. He thought, "I wonder what Phineas will say when he hears the news?"

Two years ago, Phineas had dreamed of a quick fortune. So far, the cotton gin hadn't meant anything but trouble and debts. And now—this. Would Phineas give up? He'd write to Phineas that night. If only it didn't take so long for letters to travel from New Haven to Savannah! It would be a month before he'd know what Phineas had to say.

Tim brought the letter when it came. Slowly, Eli broke the seal and opened it.

Tim couldn't wait. "Well, Mr. Whitney?"

Eli read from Phineas Miller's letter. "I will devote all my time, all my thoughts, all the money I can earn or borrow, to complete this business we have undertaken."

Tim smiled, then sobered. "It'll take all the money he can borrow, won't it? You're not earning much yet with the gin."

"That's right, Tim. We'll have to borrow. But we'll build again. We'll begin over."

Tim rumpled his hair. "You know, in a way, it would be easier to quit than to go on, wouldn't it?"

Eli thought of Tim's words many times in the next two years. They borrowed; they built again; Eli built more cotton gins. But they could never borrow enough, nor build fast enough to pay the costs of the endless trials over the patent.

Tim opened the door of the new shop late one evening in the autumn of '96. "Someone to see you, Mr. Whitney."

Captain Manders, master of the brigantine, *Sally,* bellowed, "Ahoy the shop!" and came to shake hands with Eli. He tossed a letter on the work bench. "I stopped at Savannah on my way from the West Indies. A friend sent this letter to you. I offered to bring it to save you postage. Sorry it's late."

Eli said, "I understand. Sometimes we have rough weather between Savannah and New Haven."

Captain Manders said dryly, "And sometimes we have 'rough weather' around the West Indies, too."

Eli looked at him quickly. "You think we're going to have trouble?"

The captain snorted. "I think we've already got trouble. An English ship boarded us and took off two of my sailors!"

"The English?" Eli Whitney asked. "I thought it was the French who were giving our seamen trouble."

"Hah!" Captain Manders paced up and down the floor. "If it isn't France, it's England. Straighten things out with one, you'll have trouble with the other. Mark my words! In ten years, there'll be war again, or they'll run American ships off the high seas, one or the other."

Eli studied the grim, square face. "You really believe that?"

Manders rested his fists on the work bench and leaned toward Eli. "I means this. If you're in any business that depends on exports, you'd better look around for something else to do." He straightened. "Well, I'm off. Sorry your letter was late." He went out with the rolling walk of a man who's used to a pitching deck beneath his feet.

Shaking his head, Eli turned back to his work. When the American Revolution ended, everyone had thought the nation's troubles were over. But it hadn't turned out that way.

The northern boundary, between the United States and Canada, was not settled. England still held forts and fur posts along the northern border. They claimed the right to search our ships for English-born sailors. They said we hadn't paid debts we owed to Englishmen.

All these questions needed to be settled. The thing that caused the most trouble was the way English ships treated our sailors— boarding our vessels, searching them for seamen they said had deserted from English ships.

President Washington had sent John Jay to England to try to iron out the differences. Mr. Jay had probably done the best he could do. The English had promised to get out of the forts and fur posts by a certain date. A commission was appointed to settle the dispute over the boundary, and the debts that each side owed the other.

But John Jay hadn't been able to settle the trouble on the high seas. England still laid down the law about what we could and couldn't do in our trade with the West Indies; and England still went right on stopping and searching our vessels, and seizing seamen.

Poor John Jay! What a storm there was over that treaty! Captain Manders was probably right; we did have trouble!

Tim looked after the captain. "Good thing your business doesn't depend on export, Mr. Whitney."

"But it does depend on export, Tim. Most of our cotton we gin in the South feeds the machines of England."

He opened his letter. It was from Catherine Greene. Catherine Greene Miller she was, now. She had married Phineas. And she had mortgaged Mulberry Grove.

"Phineas argued against it for days," she wrote. "Against the mortgage—not the marriage! But I have a feeling we're almost at the end of our trouble. Perhaps this money is just what is needed to tide us over."

A mortgage on Mulberry Grove! No wonder Phineas had argued against it. Catherine had had enough trouble in her life. General Greene had spent all he had to feed his men during the Revolution. If Catherine lost Mulberry Grove . . .

Eli wanted to shout, "No! You can't mortgage Mulberry Grove! You can't risk it on the future of the cotton gin!" But it was too late. The letter was dated almost two months before. Captain Manders certainly had had a rough trip.

And now, if trouble came, and exports were stopped . . . Eli's thoughts went around and around. He had to earn money some other way. Some other way . . .

Tim said, "You almost always whittle when you're thinking hard, don't you. What's that you're making?"

Eli jumped and looked down at the bit of wood in his hands. A musket, with a broken hammer.

Long ago, Hiram had said, "We don't turn out muskets like so many chair rungs on a lathe . . . handmade . . . it's the nature of muskets."

Eli said, "Tim, I want a musket."

Tim gulped. "Mr. Whitney! Don't take it that way! I know it's been hard. But you musn't—"

Eli looked at the boy, puzzled. Then he laughed. "Shoot myself? Don't worry, Tim. I just have an idea. About the nature of muskets! I want to buy one. Think you can find one for me?"

Tim hesitated. "All right . . . I reckon I can."

Tim was still worried when he brought the musket. He stood around, shuffling his feet. But when Eli took the musket apart, and began to examine the pieces, Tim finally smiled.

"Good night, Mr. Whitney."

Eli did not look up. He was regarding the nature of muskets.

The next day brought a letter from Phineas. A much more recent one than the letter from Catherine. It was desperately important, Phineas wrote, that Eli come south as soon as he could.

"I know it will mean a delay on the cotton gins," Phineas had written, "but your presence in Georgia is more important right now."

Eli said, "Maybe Captain Manders was right." He sharpened a quill. "Maybe I'd better get into another business."

Whom should he write to at the capital? Oliver Wolcott, maybe. Wolcott was a Connecticut man, proud of the mechanical genius Connecticut workmen had developed.

When he finished the letter, he addressed it to Oliver Wolcott, Secretary of the Treasury, in Philadelphia. *Philadelphia.* Eli thought of the year of the yellow-fever epidemic. He would be glad when they moved the capital to the new Federal City on the Potomac.

Tim saw Eli off when he started the long drive to Mulberry Grove. "You know what I've figured out, Mr. Whitney? You spend about a fourth of your life between here and Georgia. Just going and coming . . . I wonder what's wrong now?"

"I'll know when I get there, Tim. If a letter comes from Philadelphia, open it, and write me what it says. I won't be gone any longer than I have to." He picked up the reins.

Three weeks later, he sat with Phineas and Catherine in the high-ceilinged library at Mulberry Grove.

Phineas was haggard with worry. "Eli, someone has started a crazy rumor that our gins hurt the cotton staple. I thought you ought to be here, travel around where our gins are placed, and check. See if you can figure out anything to do." He spread a map of Georgia. "We have thirty gins scattered over the state, located at convenient places."

Eli thought of the roads he'd just traveled. "Convenient to whom?" he asked.

Phineas snapped, "The cotton planters, of course! Remember that we gin the cotton for a share of the crop."

Eli said, "I still think we'd be better off if we sold the gins outright."

"No! This is our only chance to make any money. To keep control of the machines and gin the cotton ourselves on shares!"

Eli studied the map. "It will take a while to cover all those places."

"We've got to do it. If we don't get to the bottom of that rumor, and stop it, we'll have thirty gins standing idle."

Eli thought, "Now is the time to tell them about the other business." He said, "By spring, I hope to have another business under way. I'm not giving up with the gin! Don't think that. I'll take on this other work in addition."

Catherine protested. "Eli! You can't take on anything else! You're doing three men's work now! You'll kill yourself."

Tired as he was, Eli smiled. "Don't worry

about me, Catherine, I'm strong as an ox."

Catherine begged, "Please don't think about anything else."

Eli said, "I've already asked for a contract from the government. Do you want to hear about it?"

Phineas said sullenly, "Of course."

Eli hunted for some way to make them understand. "I have an idea for getting—well—uniformity." They waited. "Let's see if I can explain it. Suppose you had two dozen boards to saw. They must be cut out to very exact measurements. You're very skilled with a saw. You cut them, and there you are."

Phineas said, "Not if I cut them! I couldn't saw to exact measurement if my life depended on it."

"You could, if I built a guide for your saw. You could, if all you had to do was to move the saw back and forth. You could, if the guide had the know-how you didn't have."

Phineas shrugged. "Look at the cost of making a guide, and the time and trouble. Why not just get a good workman in the first place?"

"What if I had ten thousand boards to saw, and there weren't enough skilled workmen?"

Eli saw in his mind's eye all the vast country filled with people—all needing things and few skilled craftsmen to fill those needs.

Phineas rubbed his chin. "Then I suppose it would be worthwhile to build the know-how into a guide."

"And suppose I wanted to build a thousand of some machine?" Eli continued.

Phineas said, "Then you'd have to have good workmen! You can only build machines, one at a time!"

Eli shook his head. "Not if I could build the know-how into guides. Not if the guides could keep the work true to measurement. Ten men could each make a different part of the machine. They could make those parts so accurately that they would fit together."

Phineas shrugged. "I suppose that's what you mean by uniformity. But think of all the trouble and the cost. What would be worth it?"

Eli answered, "Muskets for the government! Muskets made so accurately to measurement that the parts would be uniform — interchangeable. Made so that a lock from one musket would fit a thousands others."

Phineas stared. "Muskets with interchangeable parts! That's the maddest notion I've ever heard of!"

"I'm after a contract to make ten thousand flintlock muskets," Eli said.

"You! I wager you never made a musket in your life!" Phineas shouted.

Eli smiled. "I never made a cotton gin before, either, did I?"

Catherine left the men to discuss the matter together and Phineas paced the floor. "Ten thousand muskets would take you the rest of your life."

Eli shifted his gaze from the window. "I've bargained to do them in two years," he said.

"Eli, you're crazy! There aren't enough gunsmiths in the country to build ten thousand muskets in two years."

Eli agreed. "I know. I won't use gunsmiths. Just everyday mechanics. I'll build the know-how into the guides they work with."

Phineas shouted some more. After he had said everything else he could think of he bellowed, "I tell you, it's fantastic!"

Eli smiled. "You know, I've just thought of a definition of 'fantastic.' It's something that hasn't happened yet. Five years ago the cotton gin was fantastic."

Phineas smiled wryly. "But, Eli, this is

different. Think of all the machinery you'll have to build to make those muskets. What if you failed to meet your contract? You'd be ruined."

Eli said, "I don't intend to fail." He turned to the map of Georgia. "I wonder which way I should go to check on the cotton gins? To Augusta, first? You know, Phineas, those locations don't look very convenient to me."

Eli wrote again to Oliver Wolcott in Philadelphia. "I'll be in Georgia several weeks. In the event the government wants to give me a contract, a letter will reach me more quickly if it's sent to Mulberry Grove."

Then he started on horseback to check the cotton gins. It rained and his horse had to plow through the mud. The road to Augusta was bad; the road beyond Augusta was worse. Four hours out of Augusta, Eli felt as though he'd been riding two days and a night.

A horseman came toward him, and lifted a hand in greeting. "How is the road toward Augusta?"

Eli said, "Bad. I don't know how they manage to haul wagons over it at all."

The stranger said, "I wish you'd tell that to Miller and Whitney!"

"Why? What can Miller or Whitney

do about the roads?" Eli asked in surprise.

The man stormed. "They can stop trying to hog the business of ginning cotton! Will they sell their gins, so we can locate them on our plantations? Oh, no! They set up their gins in these 'convenient locations.' And we have to haul our cotton there to be ginned."

"You mean the locations aren't convenient?"

The man gave a short laugh. "Georgia! The biggest state in the union! And there are only thirty locations. Did you ever try to haul a top-heavy load of cotton over roads like these? Do you want to know what I go through just to get two hundred pounds of ginned cotton?"

Eli said, "Yes, I'd like to know. Very much."

"First," the man said grimly, " I must haul about a thousand pounds of seed cotton over roads like these to one of their 'convenient locations.' Miller and Whitney gin my thousand pounds of cotton. It makes about three hundred pounds of lint. And then — then those robbers demand a third of the lint just for ginning it! That leaves just two hundred pounds of cotton for me."

Eli said, "Are you better off now than before the gin was invented?"

The man hesitated. Then he blurted out, "That's not the point! They're robbers! I drank a toast to Eli Whitney once. But if I ever meet that man—"

From a distance someone shouted, "Mister John! Mister John!"

The man said, "I knew it! They've upset that wagon!" He whirled his horse and rode back in the direction from which he'd come. Eli followed.

The planter had guessed right. A wagon had slipped off the road and upset. Two husky Negroes were struggling with frantic, kicking mules. Eli swung from his saddle to help. The stranger stared at him. Then, he, too, dismounted.

The four men managed to calm the mules

and right the wagon. One Negro searched through the scattered load for rope and began to mend a broken rein. The other began to hoist the bags back into the wagon.

The planter mounted his horse. For the first time he smiled. "Thank you, sir," he said. "My name is Morrow, John Morrow. If you're ever near Pine Acres, stop to see us. We'd be honored to have you for a guest. Your name, sir?"

"I'm Eli Whitney."

John Morrow flushed, then whitened. He stiffened in his saddle. "Do you wish satisfaction, sir?"

"I don't understand." Eli was puzzled.

"No gentleman will take what I've said without defending his honor." The planter's knuckles were white, where he gripped the pommel of his saddle.

"A duel?" Eli shook his head. "You didn't attack our honor; you attacked our judgment. I'm glad I talked with you. I think Miller and Whitney had better change their way of handling the business end of the cotton gin. May I say 'thank you?'"

John Morrow didn't answer. He stared at Eli with bitter eyes. The Negroes had the wagon loaded again. They lashed a canvas cover over the toppling load of cotton. John Morrow wheeled his horse and rode toward Augusta. The wagonload of unginned cotton lumbered after him, swaying dangerously on the muddy road.

Eli continued on his way, thinking about the man who had offered "satisfaction" in a duel.

At dusk, it began to rain. He pushed ahead, watching for a light. At last he saw one. He turned into a long drive. Then he reined his horse sharply. A sign by the drive said, "Pine Acres."

The horse balked when Eli turned back to the road again. "Sorry, there's a limit to southern hospitality," Eli muttered, striking the animal's rump. "Pine Acres would'nt be honored to have a visit from me."

Night smothered the world with blackness. Eli gave the horse his head. He slumped in his saddle. For the first time in all the bitter grind of work and disappointment, he was completely discouraged.

"When I get back to Mulberry Grove, I'll tell Phineas we've got to change things, before it's too late," he thought. "If it's not already too late."

When he got back, he discussed the matter

with Phineas. "We've got to change our way. Somehow, we've got to increase the production of the cotton gins. And then we must sell them to the users."

Phineas began, "Now you leave the business end to—"

Eli said, "Wait!" He told Phineas about John Morrow.

Phineas listened. Then he shrugged. "Well, maybe we'll have time to build enough cotton gins to take care of the state. In a month, every gin we have will be idle. I've had word from England. The cotton merchants are refusing our cotton. I have a hunch that's where the rumor started—that our gins ruin the staple."

Eli said, "I've checked every gin. Not one has hurt the lint."

Phineas shrugged. "I know. But we're at a standstill—until we find out who's stirring trouble against us."

Eli said. "What about building gins?"

Phineas Miller's eyes shone. "Keep building them! Maybe by the time we get to the bottom of this campaign against our gins, we'll have won a case in court. Who knows? Maybe this is the dark hour before the dawn.

Next year this time, we may look back on this and smile."

Eli said, "Well, that's all I can do here, now. Any word from Philadelphia?"

"No. No word," Phineas answered.

Eli wrote again to Oliver Wolcott. "I'm leaving for the North tomorrow. I shall stop in Philadelphia to see you."

He went inland by Augusta. The warehouses of Augusta bulged with cotton, ready for shipment. As Eli passed one warehouse, he heard two men talking.

"I say the crop will pass ten million pounds this year!"

"Yes, sir! It's a new day for Georgia all right!"

Eli rode on. Strange, the tricks fate could play. Because of the cotton gin, a new day had dawned for Georgia. But he, Eli Whitney, was probably the most hated man in the state.

He crossed the Savannah and rode north. His next problem had to do with the nature of muskets.

He'd be in Philadelphia in three weeks, with luck—with good luck, that is.

King Winter

⟨⟨ TWO DAYS OUT OF PHILADEL-phia it happened. A runaway wagon on a twisting road crashed into him. Eli jumped in time. But his chaise was wrecked. He sold his horse and finished the trip to Philadelphia by stagecoach, jostling on the backless board seats.

Philadelphia at last! He wondered what news Oliver Wolcott would have. Would he smile? Or would he shake his head?

Oliver Wolcott smiled and then shook his head. "You're getting the contract, Whitney.

But I don't see how you expect to make ten thousand muskets in two years."

Eli said, "I think I can."

Wolcott still shook his head. "Our Captain Wadsworth says it's impossible. He says there aren't enough gunsmiths in America to build muskets that fast. And you know you can't train gunsmiths overnight. It takes years to make a good gunsmith."

Eli thought, "My guides will make mechanics into gunsmiths." But he didn't say it. He knew no one would believe what he meant to do. His muskets would have to speak for him.

Wolcott said, "There's a man here by the name of Sanger. He might save you some time. He imports gun barrels from Europe ready to bore."

Eli hesitated. He almost said, "No, thank you. I don't want to depend on anything coming from Philadelphia." He still remembered the months he had waited for his patent. But after all, it wasn't the fault of Philadelphia. It was because of the yellow fever.

He said, "Thank you. I'll see him."

Wolcott gave him Mr. Sanger's address. "Tomorrow's Sunday. But you'll find him at his shop bright and early Monday morning."

Sunday afternoon, Eli decided he'd take a stroll and find Mr. Sanger's place. "It shouldn't be hard to find," he thought. "I'll say that much for Philadelphia. It's easy to find your way around."

The raised footwalks, too, along both sides of the streets, were a help. No danger of being splashed by flying mud from carriage wheels. Come to think of it, though, he hadn't seen a single carriage, nor a coach. Then Eli looked at the street and understood. A heavy chain was stretched across the road. Philadelphia allowed no riding for pleasure on Sunday. He smiled. They jeered at New Haven about its Blue Laws. What about Philadelphia and and its Sunday chains?

On Chestnut Street, he crossed Fifth, and stood before the State House. Independence Hall, it was, now, where the Declaration of Independence had been signed. He thought of the wild ride of one delegate to get to the Hall in time to sign it. Caesar Rodney, of Delaware, it was, who had ridden eighty miles through blistering July heat to break the tie of the Delaware vote.

Memories of the War for Independence always came to Eli Whitney's mind in hoofbeats. Paul Revere and William Dawes, dashing through the night to warn Concord and Lexington. James Jowett, riding headlong to Monticello to warn Thomas Jefferson that the British men were coming to capture him.

Eli remembered another rider of the Revolution—Hiram Wedge, riding home from Virginia. Hiram Wedge, with his broken musket, a musket that couldn't be mended in a hurry.

"I'll do it," he told himself. "I'll make muskets another way!"

Early Monday morning, he talked to Mr. Sanger.

The man from Philadelphia said, "Ten thousand barrels in two years?" He smiled. "Well, Mr. Whitney, I'll say this. I can furnish you all the barrels you'll need. I'll deliver five hundred barrels to you in September. When you need more, I'll have them for you." Then the merchant added, "You know, your trouble will be in finding workmen."

Eli said, "I know where I can get sixty dependable men."

Mr. Sanger's smile was pitying. "Mr. Whitney, there aren't that many good gunsmiths in the country."

Eli didn't answer that. He hurried away to catch the stagecoach. It left at eight. With luck, they'd be in New York City late tomorrow afternoon.

He climbed over two benches and sat on the back one. He crowded his portmanteau between his long legs.

The passenger by him said, "Did you hear the rumor? There've been two cases of yellow fever."

In spite of himself, Eli shivered.

The passenger shrank away from him. "What's wrong? Are you sick?"

Eli said, "No, no. I was just thinking about the yellow fever of '93."

"Were you here?" The man was ready to exchange memories of that desperate time.

"I was in New Haven," Eli said.

Yes, he had been in New Haven, flushed with pride of his new invention, waiting on the patent. It had been a race against time. And he'd lost. Now, he was starting another race against time. Ten thousand flintlock muskets in two years!

The passenger said, "Well, let's hope it's just a rumor about yellow fever striking again." He swatted a mosquito. "You know what they decided caused the epidemic of '93?"

"No."

"Coffee," the man said. "A lot of coffee was rotting on the wharf." He killed another buzzing mosquito. "I'll be glad to get out of here. I haven't seen the mosquitoes so bad since '93."

The stagecoach started with a lurch.

The passenger swatted one more mosquito. "Yes, coffee, rotting on the wharf. That's what started the epidemic of yellow fever. They're very careful about that now, more orderly. They never leave stuff lying around to spoil, especially coffee."

When Eli got back to New Haven, he visited the red cliffs of rock by Mill River again. This time, old Johnathan Biddle was with him.

Eli said, "This is the land I've bought, and the dam in Mill River."

"For your gun-making, eh?" Johnathan looked at the dam. "Mighty nice head of water there, lots of power. It turned the Todd grist mill for a good many years."

Eli said, "I want to add to it. Build it higher, and—"

Johnathan's grizzled face went blank with astonishment. "Look, Mr. Whitney! That dam furnished power for a grist mill! It'll turn all the wheels you need to build muskets. Guns ain't a machine job, you know. They're hand-work."

Eli didn't argue. He just said, "I want it higher. And I want you to do the work, because I know it will be done right. After I get started, I won't have any time for break-downs."

Johnathan rubbed his chin. "It can be done. It'll take time, though, And I've got a lot of odd jobs to clear out of the way first. I don't want people after me for something I promised. I've never gone back on a promise."

Eli said, "That's another reason I want you to do the work. Set your own time, just so the dam's ready before winter sets in. I've promised first delivery on my contract next September."

Johnathan said, "Don't concern yourself, Mr. Whitney. You have my word. You'll have your dam, though why in tarnation you want it higher . . . . Well, it's your dam." He went off, muttering to himself and shaking his grizzled head.

Silas Marks argued longer about the building Eli wanted. "Look, Mr. Whitney! You just need room for gunsmiths to build muskets! Now, look! All you need is a nice little . . ."

Silas argued longer than Johnathan, but finally he, too, said, "Well, it's your building!" And he went off muttering to himself.

From dawn to dusk Eli worked in the shop on Wooster Street, building cotton gins. Before dawn and after dark he worked there, too, carving shapes out of wood.

Tim came in early one morning, before daylight. "Mr. Whitney, what are you whittling, anyhow? I've been trying to figure out."

"Patterns, Tim. You've seen founding done, haven't you? When they make a mold in sand with a wooden shape, and then run the red-hot melted iron into the hollow?"

Tim said, "Yes . . . but those patterns. I thought you were going to build muskets?"

"They're patterns for machines I'll use in building the muskets," Eli Whitney answered patiently.

Tim's eyes bulged. "I never heard of making muskets with machinery!"

"Neither did anyone else." Eli smiled. "Mr. Miller tells me it's fantastic, Tim. That means something that hasn't happened before."

"You've—you've got to get all those patterns cast—and set up all those machines— before you make any muskets?"

Eli glanced up. "Oh, these? These are just the beginning. I haven't even begun to make patterns yet!"

September came. Silas Marks and his men had the building on Mill River roofed. Johnathan stopped by to say he was ready to begin work on the dam.

"Going out there to have a look at things this morning," he said.

Eli said, "Good!"

Tim fetched him a letter from Philadelphia.

Eli said, "Good! My luck's fine this morning. Biddle is starting the work on the dam. And Sanger must have the first shipment of gun barrels on the way."

He opened the letter. Quite a long one, filling a page with fine writing. But Eli saw just two words. Yellow fever.

The letter began:

DEAR MR. WHITNEY,

In going through the papers of the late Mr. Sanger, I find he had promised to deliver five hundred gun barrels to you. I am obliged to inform you . . .

Tim was watching Eli's face as he read. "Bad news?" the young man asked at last.

Eli folded the letter. "Well, at least I know it in time." His voice was like the sound of a violin with a broken string. "I'll just have to do something else about gun barrels. That's all."

Johnathan strolled in from Mill River, his lips pursed, shaking his head. "Mr. Whitney, that dam's in bad condition. Going to take a lot of work, especially if you still think you want it higher."

"I do." Eli put the letter from Philadelphia in his pocket.

"Takes a heap of dam to stand against more water, you know."

Eli said, "Then I'll need a heap of dam. And you're the man to build it."

Johnathan went out, muttering.

Tim said, "First the gun barrels; now the dam. Maybe you said 'good' too soon."

"Old Mr. Biddle's just pulling a long face. It breaks his heart to think of anyone wasting money. And he thinks I'm wasting my money on a higher dam." Eli stood and stretched. It wouldn't do to get all tense and worried about these things. *Keep on keeping on*—that was the way to meet a challenge.

Tim felt, though he could not understand, the change in the inventor's mood. "What will you do about the gun barrels?" he asked.

"I'd better go to Salisbury about them.

That's where they make the best iron in America. Horseback's probably the best way to go."

Tim said, "You'd better ride a mountain goat. I've heard it's the best animal on those roads."

Eli managed a grin. "You're getting as gloomy as old Mr. Biddle. I'd better go to Salisbury tomorrow."

"Start for Salisbury!" Tim replied. "I wonder how long it'll take you to get there?" Then he apologized, shamefaced. "I'm sorry, Mr. Whitney. But when things start to go wrong, I get jumpy."

Eli smiled. "A bad idea, Tim. It takes a steady hand to steer through a storm."

The next morning Whitney started on

horseback toward the rugged hills of north-west Connecticut. Hills ablaze with autumn color towered higher and steeper. Streams plunged down waterfalls and over gray boulders.

Salisbury shone white and friendly against the backdrop of tawny hills. Eli stopped at the forge where Ethan Allen had cast cannon for the Army of the Revolution. That was before he marched away with his Green Mountain Boys to take Fort Ticonderoga. Ethan Allen and Hiram Wedge, Eli thought. The two most likely never met, but they had met the same fate in the same cause. The peddler came often to the inventor's mind these days.

The Forge Pond gleamed red in the glow of the iron furnaces. A man in uniform came toward Whitney. "I'm Ensign Bartry," he said. "United States Navy."

When Eli introduced himself, Bartry's face lighted. "I've heard of you, sir! In Philadelphia! The cotton gin! What brings you to Mt. Riga?"

Eli said, "Muskets. I've a contract to build ten thousand flintlocks for the army."

Bartry whistled. "You're going to put some iron into the army, aren't you?"

"Philadelphia can't supply me with gun barrels. I'm hoping Connecticut can."

Bartry smiled. "Connecticut might! She's surely been supplying some ironsides for the Navy!" His eyes glowed. "Have you seen the frigates we're building?"

"No, I haven't," Whitney said.

"They're proper ships!" Bartry sighed. "I wish I were on one. But I have to stay here for inspection duty. Well, come along, Mr. Whitney. I'll introduce you to the man who can supply you with the best iron made in America."

The ironmaster promised gun barrels. Ten thousand? He smiled at Eli the way Sanger had. He drawled, "I think we can supply you with all you'll need."

When Eli started down the steep road, Ensign Bartry said, "You should have seen us haul that anchor out of here. I forget how many yoke of oxen it took. Eight or ten, I think it was. That was the anchor for the *Constitution.* Remember that name, Mr. Whitney!" the youngster said. "I tell you, that frigate will outsail and outfight anything on the high seas!"

Eli nodded. "The *Constitution?* I'll remember."

As he mounted his horse, Bartry called, "If they ever set me free from inspection, I'll see you in New Haven! I certainly want to see how you can build ten thousand flintlocks!"

Eli started east from Salisbury. There were a dozen other things to see about, but it looked as if problems were getting solved. The gun barrels were contracted for. The building was practically ready. Old Johnathan had the work on the dam under way. Before winter set in, he'd have things started in the shop.

He turned toward New Haven, but he hadn't covered ten miles before his horse went lame. He stopped at a farmhouse to bargain for another horse.

Pleased to have a famous man like Eli Whitney on his doorstep, the farmer said, "You'd better stay the night, Mr. Whitney."

That night, Eli dreamed again of cotton. An avalanche of cotton, smothering him. Then it turned into an avalanche of snow, freezing him. He awakened, shivering. The cold was real. The wind howled; sleet lashed the windows.

At breakfast, the farmer said, "You can't start out in this, Mr. Whitney. Can't see three feet in front of your nose." He clicked his tongue against his teeth. "I never knew winter to come so early and so hard. Reckon everything is freezing solid from here to Long Island Sound. Man and boy, I've spent sixty years in these parts. I've never seen anything like this. One thing, though. An early winter means an early spring."

Eli said, "I hope so." And settled down to wait out the storm.

When Eli got back to New Haven, old Johnathan Biddle was the first man he saw.

"Mr. Whitney, I've never seen anything like it." Biddle was flushed and embarrased. "The work on your dam—I'm stopped in my tracks. I can't do a thing till spring. Not even then, I can't start. Not till the spring floods are over. Mr. Whitney, I never broke a promise before. Never."

Eli said, "I know. This early winter isn't your fault."

Old Johnathan wasn't comforted. "Not my fault. No. But it's going to put an awful hole in your plans. I'm just as sorry as I can be. But being sorry won't help."

Eli comforted the old man as best he could and went to his work. The farmer had said an early winter meant an early spring. Eli hoped he was right.

Best-Laid Plans

ELI HAD BEEN WORKING AN hour by candlelight when a pale February sun came up. Eli heard the first workman stamping snow outside the shop door.

Ben Mason entered and struggled to close the door against the wind and driving sleet. "Ever see such a winter, Mr. Whitney?"

"Never." How many times had Eli given an answer to that question these last endless months? If he had a shilling for every time, he thought wryly, he wouldn't have to be always worrying about money to pay his debts.

"I used to be glad when winter came. Short

working day, only ten hours! But this is one year I'll be glad to see spring come." Ben stamped his feet and blew on his fingers. "How are you coming with your patterns?"

"Almost done," Whitney answered.

"Going to have the fellow up Salisbury way cast them for you?"

"I don't know, Ben," Eli said. "He promised a shipment of material before the first of the year. Here it is February, and I haven't heard yet."

Ben looked out at the weather. "Probably froze up, like everybody else."

Stamping feet thundered outside the door. Ben opened it. "Come in fast!" he yelled.

Six men crowded through the door, shoving each other.

"Somebody to see you, Mr. Whitney," several voices shouted. A visitor these days was something to shout about.

Eli looked up. Ensign Bartry was with them. Eli laid down his work. "Freed from inspection?"

"Yes, I'm on my way to Philadelphia." Bartry smiled, but his eyes were troubled.

"Welcome to New Haven!" Whitney spoke warmly.

The young officer said, "You won't say that

when you hear my news. They can't do your
gun barrels for you. I told them I'd stop and
let you know."

Eli said, "Thank you, for bothering to stop."

"Oh, I wanted to come," the navy man
answered. "Frankly, I'm curious about your
works. The armory, I mean. How are things
coming?"

"They're standing still." Eli told Bartry
what the early winter had done to his plans.

Bartry said, "That's bad. You might try
Canaan for your barrels. Forbes, there, has a
fine reputation. He's always on time with his
work. At least, that's what everyone says of
him."

Eli thought, "That would be a pleasant
change—something on time!" He said, "I've
heard of him. I'm planning to take my pat-

terns to him for casting. He might do the gun barrels in addition."

Bartry looked at the odd-shaped patterns. "Whew! First cotton gins! Then muskets! And now another project!"

"No. These are patterns for machinery to use in making the muskets."

Bartry looked puzzled, then smiled stiffly. "I didn't mean to ask questions out of turn. I'm not asking what your other project is sir."

Eli said, "But I told you. Engines for making muskets."

Bartry didn't answer for a moment. Then, with his same stiff little smile, he said, "Well, I must be going. Good luck on your trip to Canaan. Travel's not too bad right now, with a sled. Don't hurry it, though. If snow threatens, stop. Don't get caught in a blizzard."

Bartry bowed and went out. Ben Mason helped him with the door. He turned back. "More snow. You'd think it'd snow itself out, wouldn't you? If this keeps up, we'll have some nasty spring floods. Floods will hold up work on that dam."

Eli was still staring at the door through which Bartry had disappeared. "You know," he said slowly, "I could swear he didn't believe me about machines for making muskets."

Silence thickened in the Wooster Street shop. Eli looked up at his workmen. Their faces were carefully blank.

"Look, Mr. Whitney," Ben drawled, "we ain't asking what those patterns are for. Figure it ain't any of our business. But any fool knows you ain't going to use that stuff to make flintlock muskets."

Eli opened his mouth to answer. But what was the use? Nobody was going to believe him until the muskets were made. It was fantastic. It hadn't happened yet.

He shrugged into his coat. "Take care of things, will you, Ben? I'm going to breakfast."

When Eli's patterns were done, he took them to Cannan, to the man "who was always on time." Mr. Forbes smiled at Bartry's words about his fine reputation.

" 'Always on time' is what I try to be, Mr. Whitney. Just now, our works are frozen up. But we'll try to cut out our wheels tomorrow and get to work. When we are going again, I can do your work in two weeks." He studied the patterns. "I've never cast any like these before."

Eli said, "Probably not. These are my own invention."

He didn't explain further; no one was going to believe he'd make muskets by machinery.

Mr. Forbes said, "Anything else we can do for you?"

"I'm going to need several tons of iron, of the best quality. Any idea where I could get it?"

"Yes. Lowman. He has a reputation, too, for being on time!"

Eli returned from Canaan, cheered. And one March day he heard a pleasant sound. The drip, drip of melting ice! The farmer had been right! They'd have an early spring!

But that night, the wind howled again. A blizzard came in from the West. March shivered into April.

A letter came from Forbes. In spite of everything he could do, not a wheel was turning. Winter had defeated him.

A letter came from Lowman. Not a pound of ore had been dug. And now forage for the oxen was almost gone. Winter had defeated him, too.

Old Johnathan Biddle came to Eli. "Mr. Whitney, I'm stumped. No forage for the teams. We can't work the animals without food."

"I know." Eli was desperate. "I'll pay double

the usual rates for teams! More, if I have to."

"It won't help, Mr. Whitney." Johnathan Biddle rubbed his knuckles. "You can't feed oxen money. They have to have food. If this keeps up, I don't know when we'll get that dam done."

"It can't keep up much longer, Johnathan."

But on the first of June, Eli sent a letter to Oliver Wolcott, explaining the state of things. Not a wheel was turning yet; not a single casting had come from Forbes; not a pound of iron had come from Lowman. Eli's money was gone. He'd have to have further advances from the government.

Perhaps Oliver Wolcott would understand. He was a New Englander. He'd know what this long, bitter winter had meant. But could he make the War Department understand?

Four thousand muskets were due in September. Just three months away. And there weren't going to be any four thousand muskets, not even four hundred muskets, nor forty, nor even four.

A year of frantic work had gone by. And there wasn't going to be a single musket from the Whitney Armory. Not in September, there wasn't. Not a one!

"Your Obedient Servant"

OLIVER WOLCOTT DID UNDERstand about the delay. Again and again he got more money from the government for Eli; a thousand now; five thousand another time.

At last the dam was done; castings arrived from Canaan; tons of iron arrived. Strange machines filled the shop on Mill River. Men came to the shop and began to work.

Here a man laid a small shape into a guide and began to file, without stopping to measure. The guide told him when the measurements were right. He could work without stopping.

Over and over again, the mechanic turned out pieces exactly alike.

Here a man fastened a steel plate, with holes bored in it, over a piece of iron and began to drill. There was no stopping to measure. The guide told him where the holes must be. No stopping! Over and over again! Pieces drilled exactly alike!

But there were no muskets. No man made muskets. Each man turned out odd pieces, exactly alike.

A delegation of men from Germany came to the shop. They understood Mr. Whitney had gathered together an amazing number of gunsmiths. Perhaps he could also produce guns for their government? Their glances darted around the shopful of machinery.

But where, one asked in broken English, was Mr. Whitney making guns?

Eli explained. He was not building muskets here, one at a time. He was manufacturing muskets. Each of his workmen was working at a different task. Some parts of the musket weren't being made yet. When all the parts were being made, he would assemble muskets —put them together.

The man explained to his companions in

German.   They laughed heartily and went away.

A French officer came next. His government was interested in buying guns. He stared blankly at the machinery.

"But, Monsieur Whitney, you do not understand! It is the muskets I have come to see."

Eli explained again. The French officer did not laugh. He was full of pity.

"Monsieur Whitney, I think you have never before made firearms."

He went away. Just beyond the door, he shrugged his shoulders. Eli saw, and smiled grimly. So the Frenchman shrugged off the idea of making muskets a new way? Why wouldn't he? After all, there were no muskets, were there? Just a building full of strange machines that seemed to have nothing to do with guns. Any fool knew that the making of muskets was handwork.

Eli felt the challenge. He must get every part in production. If he did not, the contract would be canceled before he had produced a single gun. For a month, two months, he must forget the cotton engine shop on Wooster Street; he must spend every possible minute, day and night, at the armory.

A letter came from Phineas that day. The

English were buying cotton again. English manufacturers were begging for more and more cotton. Eli must bend every effort to increase production of the cotton gins!

Eli worked until midnight in the Wooster Street shop, making plans, writing orders for the men who worked on the cotton gins. Then he tramped the two miles to the armory and unlocked the door.

When Tim Horner came to the armory about two in the morning, Eli was still working.

Eli said, "Hello, Tim. Don't you ever sleep?"

"That's just what I was going to ask you. Mr. Whitney, I've watched you work for over five years now. Isn't it about time you—slowed down a little bit?"

Eli looked around the armory. "Tim, I've just begun to work. This next year, I'll really be busy."

Some way, somehow, more cotton gins had to be made. And they were. They went south on ships. They went south on wagons, drawn by oxen.

Some way, somehow, muskets had to be completed. And they were. When Captain Wadsworth, in charge of the inspection of muskets for the War Department, came to the armory, Eli gave him a completed flintlock to examine.

The captain knew firearms. His fingers moved swiftly, taking the musket apart, putting it together.

"Excellent work, Mr. Whitney. I must say, excellent work."

But the captain's tone left something hanging in the air between them. He did not say in words, but Eli could hear him thinking: *"Excellent work, Mr. Whitney, but where are ten thousand muskets? Your time is almost up, Mr. Whitney. Where are the guns?"*

A few nights after Captain Wadsworth's visit, Eli sat alone in the armory and held his head in his hands. Ten thousand muskets in two years? He had been wrong, miserably wrong. It had taken him two years just to get his plant ready for production.

Excellent work — *but where were ten thousand muskets?*

The parts were exact; they were interchangeable. The guides took care of that. But men could still make mistakes and cause delays. They might run drills too fast, overheat them, and ruin them. They might let a blast of air at the forge strike the heated iron. They might let scrap fall into a mold. Yes, no matter how hard they tried, they still made mistakes.

If he could just spend every minute at the armory. But, two miles away, was the factory on Wooster Street, where men made the cotton gins. And here problems had to be solved too.

"I ought to be twins," Eli told himself.

Tim Horner came to the armory with three letters.

A letter from Phineas said that Eli's presence in the South was needed as soon as possible.

The second letter was from the new capital at Washington. Some men in Congress were threatening to have his patent on the cotton gin canceled. They argued it wasn't fair for any one man to control anything so important as the cotton gin.

The third letter was from Washington, too. There was grave danger that Eli's contract for muskets would be canceled, unless he could come to Washington. Could Mr. Whitney give satisfaction in the matter of the long delay in carrying out the terms he had bargained for?

"Being twins wouldn't help," Eli groaned.

"What will you do, Mr. Whitney?" Tim asked.

"I'll go to Washington first and talk to the War Department," Eli decided. "I'll try to make them understand."

*   *   *

The big room in Washington seemed full of haze. The eyes that watched Eli were black holes in hazy faces. The voices that hammered questions seemed far away.

"I'm tired; that's all," Eli told himself. "Just tired." He tried to listen, tried to see the faces more clearly.

One figure seemed clear in the fog. A lean man, who dangled long legs and slouched in his chair. The man's face was clear, a sharp, narrow face, with deep-set eyes. His voice was clear, a quiet voice that spoke with the accent of Virginia.

Time and again, as Eli answered questions, he felt the eyes of the Virginian on him. Those understanding eyes gave him courage to try to explain.

But Eli knew he wasn't talking well. The faces in the fog were not convinced. He had promised to carry out a contract in two years,

and he had failed. Nothing he said seemed to explain.

Perhaps his muskets could speak for him. He went to the long table where the boxes lay. Dozens of boxes, filling the long table.

"Each of these boxes," he said, "contains uniform samples of one part of this flintlock musket I'm making. With your permission, I'll choose any sample part from each box . . ."

Swiftly, he chose the parts and assembled a musket. Whitney looked around the silent room. He saw the men looking at each other. They were not yet convinced. Perhaps they thought the parts were marked, that there was some secret distinction which helped in assembling the parts of the weapon.

An officer stood. His eyes flashed; his jaw was outthrust. "Are you willing for me to try to assemble a musket from those sample parts?"

"Of course." Whitney breathed more freely now.

The officer strolled to the table that held the boxes. He chose the parts rapidly, and began to assemble the musket. Halfway through he turned to stare at Eli.

"But—but—this is fantastic."

Eli said, "Not fantastic. Not by my definition. For me, fantastic is something that hasn't happened yet."

He heard a quiet chuckle. The soft-voiced Virginian was smiling at him.

Captain Wadsworth stirred. "There is no doubt about the excellence of Mr. Whitney's work. His skill is not to be questioned. But, as I said in my report, there is more here to amaze the curious than to be of practical use."

The tall Virginian reached in his pocket. "Gentlemen," he said, "I'd like to read to you from the copy of a letter I wrote fifteen years ago, when I was in France." His long fingers smoothed the paper. "This is a report of something I'd seen that summer in Paris." He read in quiet accents:

An improvement is made here in the construction of muskets which it may be interesting to Congress to know. It consists in making every part of them so exactly that what belongs to any one may be used for every other musket. As yet, the inventor has completed only the lock of the musket. I went to the workman. He presented me with the parts of fifty locks taken to pieces. I put several together, myself, and they fitted in the most perfect fashion. But it will be two or three years before he will be able to furnish any quantity.

The man looked up from his paper. "Le Blanc was the workman's name. He was willing to come to America. I hoped our Congress would be interested. But they weren't. They probably thought his idea was—" he smiled at Eli, "—fantastic."

He folded his paper. "I don't know what became of Le Blanc. Perhaps the Revolution in France put an end to his experiment."

The Virginian put the paper back in his pocket. "Le Blanc's country failed him. They didn't support him with the funds and the faith he needed to complete his idea. So they lost his great gift."

The man's warm glance swept over the faces around him. "Now, gentlemen," he said, "one of our countrymen has thought of his same idea. He has carried it much further than Le Blanc did. He has proved it can be a success. He has made one mistake. He has mistaken the time it would take to carry out his plan. We are getting upset over the delay. We are quibbling about funds and faith to complete this great idea. We are in danger of repeating the mistake France made. We are in danger of losing the second great gift Eli Whitney has, for his country."

A man in uniform began to talk, then another. Eli sagged in his chair. He knew the fight was won. He would get the time and the money he needed to complete the contract.

Through the haze of tiredness, Eli looked at the smiling face across the table. He remembered the first letter he had had from the Virginian, when he'd written about the cotton gin. He thought of the simple friendliness of the letter, and the way it had been signed:

"Your obedient servant,

THOMAS JEFFERSON."

World Beyond Roads

TIM HORNER HAD SOMETHING on his mind. He'd had something on his mind for the last two weeks. Now he meandered about the armory, picking up things and laying them down.

"Mr. Whitney, remember when you came back to New Haven? I was just a youngster then, a very unhappy boy, in 1793."

"Yes, Tim." Whitney looked at the husky young man and wondered what he had on his mind.

"The yellow fever," Tim said.

"I remember."

"I'd lost my whole family. Everyone." Tim hurried to get his words out. "I was mighty alone. You certainly were a friend. I'll never forget that."

Eli laid down his work. "What's on your mind, Tim? Are you wanting to leave me? Work somewhere else?"

Tim whirled. "Oh, no, Mr. Whitney! I want to work for you the rest of my life. I—I —just—wanted you to be best man at my wedding."

"Then why in tarnation didn't you say so?" Eli chuckled. "You've had me worried for two weeks!"

"I—just couldn't get around to it. I thought maybe you didn't think much of marriage."

Eli said, "I guess I've just been too busy and too much in debt to think of marriage, Tim. If I ever get this contract for muskets completed, I might think about getting married. Ten thousand flintlocks at thirteen dollars and forty cents comes to a lot of money. I ought to have enough left out of that to think of marrying. If we ever win a suit in Georgia, and stop the pirating of the cotton gin, then we might make some money on it. Then I could think of getting married. But not now."

"But you will be my best man?" Tim said.

"I'll be proud to, Tim, if I'm not on my way south again, when the wedding day comes."

"The wedding's tomorrow," Tim said. "I've been two weeks trying to tell you about it."

Eli grinned. "Because you had a notion I didn't think much of marriage?"

Tim nodded. "I hadn't thought about debts and the way you work. You know, Mr. Whitney, I'm glad I'm not a great man—doing something my country will never forget! Doing something great for your country certainly costs a big price." He opened the door. "Good night, Mr. Whitney! Helen's waiting for me!"

Tim went out, whistling. The door closed, and Eli was alone. He stared after Tim a moment, then shrugged. He studied a piece of the musket with narrowed eyes and began to design another piece of machinery.

Two letters came for Eli the next morning. The one from Phineas said it was very important that Eli come to Savannah as soon as possible. The other was from Thomas Jefferson, now President of the United States. When Eli Whitney traveled south again, the President hoped Eli would stop to see him.

Tim whistled over the letter from Jefferson.

"Just think of being asked to drop in and see the President! Like you were — well — neighbors."

The whole wedding party had heard of the letter from Jefferson. Young Mrs. Timothy Horner held hands with her husband and smiled up at Eli.

"It must be exciting, Mr. Whitney, to be great. Tim, do you think you'll ever be great?"

Tim Horner looked at Eli and then at his bride. "I hope not. I'd miss a lot."

Henrietta Edwards, Judge Pierpont Edwards' daughter, joined them. She cocked her head and smiled up at Eli. "Congratulations to you, Eli Whitney! Please, may I shake the hand that is going to shake the hand of the President?"

Eli was embarrassed and everyone laughed.

"Father is thrilled about it, too," Henrietta declared. "He wondered if you could come to dinner tomorrow night, just to celebrate. Please say 'yes'."

Before Eli could answer, Judge Edwards came through the crowd. "Will you say a good word for me in Washington, Eli?" Chuckling, he looked down at his daughter. "I think Henrietta is going to use this as an excuse to have you for dinner. She's been hinting to me for the last half hour."

Henrietta said, "Father! You beast!" And fled.

Eli explained that he was leaving immediately on a trip south. "I'm sorry I can't be with you for dinner tomorrow night."

Judge Edwards cocked his eyebrow. "Tell Henrietta. She's the one who'll be disappointed." Still chuckling, he strolled away.

But Eli couldn't find young Mistress Edwards anywhere. He left the wedding party early. He must be on his way. There was the stop to make in Washington.

* * *

Washington was a swamp of muggy heat. No wonder the congressmen growled when the capital was moved from Philadelphia. Philadelphia was the largest and most up-to-date city in the country. And Washington— well—Pierre L'Enfant's plan was supposed to be very fine. Some day, perhaps, Washington would be a handsome city. But the Federal City didn't look like much yet, as Eli drove to the Executive Mansion.

Meriweather Lewis, the President's secretary, greeted Eli eagerly. "I hoped I'd have a chance to talk to you, Mr. Whitney. You've traveled a great deal, haven't you?"

"Just back and forth," Eli said.

"Do you know anything about navigation?"

"No. I've done all my traveling on land. Why, Mr. Lewis?" Eli said. "Are you thinking of going to sea?"

"Not exactly." Mr. Lewis fingered the pages of the heavy book he was reading. "But if a man—well—if a man took a long journey by land . . ."

Eli chuckled. "Our roads aren't that bad!"

Lewis smiled and was serious again. "But a world beyond roads . . ."

"You mean west?" Eli asked. "Our roads reach farther west all the time; the Wilderness Road; the National Road. Clear on the very western border of our United States, there's a road. And there's the Natchez Trace, along the Mississippi River, from Nashville, south."

Lewis nodded slowly. "Yes, there's even the Natchez Trace. . . ."

A door opened and Thomas Jefferson smiled down at Eli.

Eli jumped to his feet. "Mr. President . . ."

The President said, "The name is still 'Jefferson.' Come in, Whitney. Sit down."

The President slouched at his desk, and

shoved aside the map he had spread before him. "You're on your way south again?"

Eli nodded. "Something about the cotton gin."

"Meantime, the manufacture of muskets?" Jefferson asked soberly.

Eli sighed. "It will be slowed down until I get back. No matter how carefully I plan, it happens. I know I've been very slow with the muskets. These never-ending suits over the cotton gin."

The President said, "Have you ever considered letting Mr. Miller handle everything in the South? It's just a suggestion, Whitney. You know the situation better than I do. But—" he smiled to soften the words "—the quantity of muskets we're getting does leave something to be desired, doesn't it?"

Eli said again, "It's these suits over the cotton gin."

The President nodded. "And all your trouble there started because of the delay on your patent. And I was Secretary of State then."

"It wasn't your fault, sir," Eli said. "It wasn't anybody's fault. It was the yellow fever. I've never blamed you for the delay. I've always remembered the first letter I had from you, about the cotton gin. Ever since, I've always felt . . ." He stopped. It was hard to remember that this tall, soft-spoken, plainly dressed man was President of the United States, and, more than any one other American, the founder of our liberties.

"You've felt that I was your friend?" Jefferson said. "I'm glad if you can feel that— after the long delay on the patent."

"It was because of the yellow fever," Eli insisted. "I've always felt that you did everything in your power."

"*Power* . . ." Jefferson's eyes had a seeing-through-you look that reminded Eli of Hiram Wedge. "Power. . . . Right now I'm straining my power to the cracking point."

The President looked at the map on his desk, and started to say something else. But his secretary, Meriweather Lewis, knocked and opened the door. There was another caller to see the President.

Eli said good-by. "I'll talk to Phineas Miller about taking over the management of everything in the South," he promised. "I'll either write to you, or see you on my return."

Jefferson nodded and smiled. His eyes strayed to the map again.

Eli puzzled over his visit. Young Mr. Lewis

—what did he mean by a world beyond roads? The President—what did he mean by straining his power to the cracking point?

Somehow, the journey south seemed longer than ever. And, Eli thought, so far, every trip south had been a waste of time. A month, six weeks, two months of time would be chopped out of production, and nothing would be gained.

"I'll have to have an understanding with Phineas," Eli told himself. "He'll have to take care of things in the South. I'm too far behind with work in New Haven."

By the time Eli reached Mulberry Grove, he had decided just what he'd say to Phineas. He turned into the three-shaded drive.

Catherine must have heard him coming. She was on the long veranda, waiting. She looked pale and worn as she reached out both hands to Eli.

"You haven't heard, have you, Eli? Phineas —it was very sudden . . ." She couldn't go on. She didn't need to. Eli realized that Phineas Miller was dead.

Catherine buried her face in her hands. "It was too much for him, Eli. The struggles, the disappointments, the delays. And now, it's all on your shoulders. And you have your

other work, too.   Oh, Eli, what will you do?
You can't carry this burden alone!   It will
break you, too!"

"You mustn't worry about me, Catherine,"
Eli said gently.   "I've good men in the factory
up north, and at the armory.   And these trips
are not a burden; they just make a pleasant
change."

Catherine cocked her head to look at him.
For a moment she showed a flash of her old
spirit.   "Eli Whitney, you're a poor liar!"

The next weeks were so busy that Eli had
little time to remember about his visit with
Jefferson.   Once he wondered how much more
delay there would have to be about his contract for muskets, now.   But he had no time to
puzzle over Meriweather Lewis's "world beyond roads," or the power the President had
strained to the cracking point.

He and Catherine worked early and late
over the confusion of Phineas Miller's records.
It was no easy matter to untangle the facts
that were on paper, or to guess the facts that
Phineas had carried in his head.   Eli was on
his way north again when the news rocked
the country.   Thomas Jefferson had purchased the territory called Louisiana from
Napoleon Bonaparte for fifteen million dollars!

The Mississippi River was the outlet to the sea from all the western territory. When Spain held the land beyond the mouth of the river, they had agreed that Americans could use New Orleans as a port from which to export and import goods. Then Napoleon got back the part of the territory that had belonged to France.

Jefferson had felt that something had to be done to keep the Mississippi River open for western trade. He sent James Monroe to France to try to buy New Orleans and the land around the river mouth. The bargaining dragged on and on. Then all at once, Napoleon offered to sell all the land claimed by France, the territory called Louisiana.

At every stop on his journey north Eli heard the tale told around the tavern tables. This, he thought, was what the President had meant by "straining his power to the cracking point." But there was no quibbling among the people. . . . Thomas Jefferson had done a great thing!

The only question people asked was how much land we'd bought. What did Louisiana Territory really consist of? And the people would soon have the answer to that one, too, when Meriweather Lewis and his friend Mr. Clark got back. No wonder, Eli chuckled, Mr.

Lewis was thinking in terms of navigation for his journey to a "world beyond roads!"

When Eli got back to New Haven, Captain Manders was in port—just returned from the West Indies. "So we've doubled the size of our country, have we, Mr. Whitney?"

Eli said, "I wonder why Napoleon sold it to us?"

The burly sea captain smiled grimly. "Yellow fever. If it hadn't been for yellow fever, we'd have Napoleon right in our backyard. He had an army in the West Indies, all ready to set up housekeeping, you might say. Then yellow fever struck. His men died like flies. Yes, sir, we ought to set up a statue to yellow fever. It did a better job of fighting for us than we could do right now."

"You still think we'll have trouble?" Eli said.

The captain snorted. "Whitney, we've got trouble or I'm a liar!" He was silent a moment; then he shrugged off whatever he was thinking. "I hear your partner died. You've got the whole thing on your shoulders—New Haven to Savannah. Cotton gins and muskets. Mr. Whitney, you've got trouble, too!"

"--Less Advances"

◷ IT WAS THREE YEARS LATER, in 1807, when Tim Horner said, "Mr. Whitney! I've just been checking! By next Wednesday we'll complete this contract!"

"Yes." Eli looked up wearily. "In eight years, instead of two."

But Tim was not to be put off. "Ten thousand muskets! A hundred and thirty-four thousand dollars. That ought to ease things up a little for you," he said.

The older man corrected, "You mean one hundred and thirty-four thousand dollars—less advances."

"That's so. . . . How much money have they advanced to you?"

Eli shook his head. "I've lost count. It's all in the records. I'll write to Washington, now. I'll tell them the final shipment will be made next Wednesday, and tell them where they can reach me in Savannah."

Tim's face fell. "Savannah? But—"

"Another trial." There was a hint of bitterness in the inventor's voice now—of bitterness and discouragement.

Tim flushed. "We were planning a surprise party for you! A dinner! Helen and I. And Henrietta Edwards was coming. She said she'd rather celebrate the completion of your contract than anything she could think of."

Eli smiled. "Odd, isn't it, that a girl should care about an arms contract?"

For a moment Tim was silent. Then he blurted out. "Don't you know what Henrietta Edwards thinks of you?"

"Probably Mistress Edwards thinks that I'm a down-at-the-heels inventor who took eight years to complete a contract he promised in two years. A down-at-the-heels inventor who hasn't made enough out of the cotton gin to buy a new pair of shoes." Eli sharpened a quill. "I'd better write that letter to Washington."

"If we'd move that dinner up to tomorrow night?" Tim suggested.

Eli shook his head. "I'm leaving in the morning. This trial may be important."

Tim said, "How many suits have you had?"

"Somewhere around sixty.'

"How many suits have you lost?" Tim pressed the point.

"All of them," Eli answered shortly.

"How much longer are you going to keep this up?" Tim asked. Somewhere, he thought, there must be a limit.

Eli glanced up at the scowling young man. "Why, until I win, of course." He dipped his quill in ink and began to write.

Tim rumpled his hair. "Mr. Whitney, you've missed every celebration, every holiday, every—*You've missed everything!*"

Strange how a chance remark would stick in your head and say itself over and over. All the long drive south, Eli heard Tim's words beating in his head, like a tune, singing itself over and over.

Even when he sat in the courtroom, he couldn't get Tim's words out of his mind.

You've missed everything. He tried to listen to what the lawyers were saying, but he couldn't.

It seemed to him that the argument had been going on for years, perhaps because it was the same argument. This time it was the man named Holmes, who was claiming that Eli's invention was not original; that it was not practical or useful. He even swore that his gin, using saws instead of wire teeth, was a new invention.

You've missed everything. You've missed . . .

Judge Johnson was speaking. Eli jerked himself out of his memories and tried to listen to what the judge was saying.

"Cotton has furnished clothing to mankind before the age of Herodotus. . . ."

Phineas had said something like that the first night they talked of the cotton gin. "Men have tried for two thousand years to seed this green-seed cotton, and they have failed. . . . That's why there are millions in your invention."

Millions . . . Eli's collar was frayed, his trousers worn, and his shoes couldn't go to the shoemaker to be mended again.

There was a stir in the courtroom. Judge Johnson's voice was a whiplash.

"With regard to the usefulness of this discovery, this court considers it a waste of time to dwell on the subject. Our debts have been paid off; our capital has increased; our lands have grown three times over in value. We cannot measure the debt which the country owes this invention."

A new day for Georgia. How long ago had he heard a man say that in Augusta? A man standing in front of a warehouse bulging with cotton? Ten years had gone by since then. Ten years ago it had been a new day for Georgia. But it hadn't been a new day for him, Eli thought. It had been just ten more years of debts and work.

Another stir in the courtroom brought Eli's thoughts back. The judge was talking about the saw-toothed gin.

"What does it amount to, except a more convenient way of making the same thing? Every idea of Mr. Whitney's is preserved. The cylinder, the iron tooth, the breastwork and brush and all the merit of this discovery. *Let the decree for perpetual injunction be entered.*"

Eli Whitney had won! Thirteen years of struggle and debt and endless travel on endless roads north to south. Sixty cases dragging through courts year after year! And he had won! This was the meaning of Judge Johnson's decree.

Eli left the courtroom so lighthearted he felt dizzy. After all these years of driving work, he had won two battles. He'd completed the contract for muskets; he'd won an injunction against the pirating of his patent.

Now he could make money on the cotton gin! No more thousands had to be spent on court cases. For the first time in long years, Eli felt he could think about himself and a life of his own. He'd stop on the way north, he decided, and get some new clothes. He'd return to New Haven like an old-time cavalier. He'd have that celebration dinner, too, with Tim and Helen, and Henrietta Edwards, too.

Henrietta. . . . Odd how many pleasant memories he had of her when he stopped to think. Yes, he'd have her to dinner.

As he walked toward the tavern, Eli passed a huddle of men. The men glanced sidelong at him and stopped talking. Then, when he had passed, they began to talk again. The voice of one man carried.

"Don't worry. Whitney's patent has almost run out. A patent only runs fourteen years. It

won't be long before we'll have free rein with
the cotton gin."

The life of the patent! Eli had forgotten
about that. A patent gave the inventor all
rights in his invention for fourteen years.
Then anyone could copy his invention.

He'd won in court, but he wasn't going to
have long to enjoy the victory. Not unless
Congress would extend the life of his patent.
They could do that. An act of Congress
would extend his patent for a few years, long
enough for him to make a little profit on his

invention. But would the Congress act?

The spring went out of Eli's step. He walked slowly to the tavern.

A letter waited for him there, from the War Department. His contract for ten thousand muskets was completed. A balance was due him on the hundred and thirty-four thousand dollars—less advances. A balance of twenty-four hundred dollars and forty-eight cents!

Eli had always been quick at ciphering. Those eight years of frantic work had brought him a profit of exactly three hundred dollars and six cents a year.

His chaise was waiting. He'd better go. It was a long way to New Haven. He wouldn't have to take time to buy new clothes, and there wouldn't be any celebration dinner. There'd be nothing to celebrate with Tim and Helen and Henrietta.

Henrietta. . . . Tim had said, "Don't you know what she thinks of you?"

He'd been right when he answered, "That I'm a down-at-the-heels inventor." That's what he was. There was no reason for the young and pretty daughter of Judge Edwards to think anything of Eli Whitney.

It was a long road yet. The kind of road a man traveled alone.

The Interrupted Dream

⊂Ξ ELI WAKENED WITH A START and stared into the darkness. Men were talking just outside his open window. Where was he? New Haven? Savannah? Philadelphia? Washington? That was it. Washington . A little inn in Washington. His room was on the first floor, and his window opened on the veranda. He wished he could close the window, but a summer night in Washington was too hot for that. He had been wakened by the confusion of four men talking at once.

"And I was having such a pleasant dream," he muttered.

171

Yes, a very pleasant dream! In his dream, his patent had been renewed. He'd hurried back to New Haven with the good news, hurried back to tell Henrietta Edwards about it. In this dream he'd talked to Henrietta without a bit of trouble. He'd explained to her all about why he had never married, that there had never been enough money. He had spoken out boldly, without being embarrassed at talking to such a young and pretty girl.

"All the cotton gin has ever earned has gone to pay debts, Henrietta," he'd said. "But now the patent is renewed. Now I'll earn something with the cotton gin. My lean days are over. I can plan for a home of my own, now. Henrietta, will you—would you—"

Even in his dreams, Eli had stumbled a little when he tried to talk of marriage. But Henrietta had seemed to understand. She had looked up at him.

"Eli," she'd said. . . . "Ever since I first saw you, when I was a little girl—too young for such a famous man to notice—"

And then the rumble of voices had wakened him. They might at least have kept still until he'd learned what Henrietta was going to say!

Outside the window, the argument grew louder.

A coarse, challenging voice said, "You wouldn't dare! You'd be a traitor to the people who sent you to Congress! You wouldn't dare!"

"But I will dare." The second voice was well-bred, quieter, but every word was clear. The speaker might as well have been standing by Eli's bed. "Judge Johnson's decree gave Whitney the right to his invention."

Eli sat up. Who was defending his rights to renew his patent? He'd heard that voice somewhere before.

The older man growled, "But why? The patent law gives an inventor the benefits of his patent for a fourteen-year period. What right does Whitney have to more than that?"

"He hasn't had any benefits yet. Just trouble."

The older man grumbled, "Oh, I know he's had a little trouble. But let's talk cold dollars and cents! Whitney made plenty out of that cotton gin!"

"Cold dollars and cents?" the quiet voice said. "Then let's talk cold dollars and cents. I know how much money he's made. I went to the trouble to find out. If Eli Whitney were paid just half a cent a pound for the cotton seeded by his gins in one year, it would be more money than he's ever earned with his invention."

"Humph." The older man seemed stumped for a moment. Then he muttered, "But if Congress renews the patent, he'll get too rich. No man has a right to make that much money off his country."

The quiet voice said, "The cotton gin has meant at least a hundred million dollars to our country. Am I being a traitor when I say the planters in the southern states owe this man something? Yet we balk at renewing his patent for a few years." A chair scraped. "Good night, sir," the voice said. "I'm going to bed."

Eli lay back, smiling into the darkness. Where had he heard that voice before?

The next morning his mood was a happy one. As he dressed, he was still trying to place the voice. Then someone tapped on his door. "Mr. Whitney? I'd like to see you, sir." It was the quiet man again.

"Come in! The door's unlocked," Eli called.

The man entered, tall, slim, handsome in his long-skirted coat, high-topped beaver hat carried in his hand. "You won't remember me, Mr. Whitney—"

Eli smiled. "But I do. John Morrow, of Pine Acres."

The southerner shook hands. "I don't know how to say this. It's about your patent, sir."

Eli flushed. "You don't need to say it. It was too hot to close windows last night. Mine opens on the veranda."

John Morrow's glance whipped toward the

window. "Oh, I see. You heard us talking last night." He smiled and then sobered. "I'm afraid it's a lost cause, Mr. Whitney. This attempt to renew your patent. But I'm going to fight for it. If we lose, I'll still be prouder of myself than if I'd been on the winning side."

"Thank you." *A lost cause;* Eli stored the words in his mind as you'd put pennies in your purse and close it tight.

"Mr. Whitney," John Morrow said, "you asked me once if I were better off since the cotton gin was invented. I didn't answer you, but I was. We all were. We are now. Your cotton gin has covered the South with a blanket of white. I remember, just before I heard of the cotton gin, I had fifty slaves. I was about to sell three boys. I couldn't afford to keep them. I thought slavery was dying out in the South. Now I have more than a hundred slaves."

That was something Eli hadn't counted on. The cotton gin had been invented to give people more goods—a better life. It had done that, but it had made slavery profitable, too, and that was not good.

Yes, slavery was increasing in the South. The feeling against it was increasing in the

North. Eli wondered what the end would be.
John Morrow said, "If you'd breakfast with
me, sir, Pine Acres would be honored."

At the table, John Morrow lifted his coffee
cup. "I drank a toast to you once before. I'll
repeat it now. *To Eli Whitney!* And may you
have good luck. May your patent be renewed."

For the first time, Eli began to have hopes.
John Morrow was a southerner. He had been
very bitter about the cotton gin at one time.
Now he had changed. True, there was a
group in Congress fighting against him. But if
enough men saw it John Morrow's way . . .

John Morrow was the last man to tell Eli
good-by, when the decision had come and he
was ready to start back to New Haven. "I'm
sorry about the patent. More sorry than I
can say, that your application was lost."

"Thank you," Eli said. "I'll never forget
what you tried to do."

"What will you do now, Mr. Whitney?"

Whitney shrugged. "I have another contract for arms for the government. I'll begin
working on it. I'll keep on till it's done." He
smiled grimly. "I'll be too busy to waste time
mourning about the cotton gin."

"What about your wife?" John Morrow
asked. "How will she feel?"

"I have no wife," Eli said. "No one to worry."

"Oh . . . well, in a way that's better, isn't it? One hates to disappoint his wife." At Pine Acres Lucinda Morrow would be waiting to hear the decision of Congress. She at least would be disappointed. She believed the patent should have been renewed.

"Yes, it's better," Eli said. "And, thank you again, John Morrow."

"Thank *you*, Eli Whitney! For benefits received!" John Morrow walked away, slim and handsome in his high-topped beaver hat.

Alone, Eli thought of his interrupted dream. "A good thing they woke me up," he said, "before Henrietta said 'Yes.'"

There was nothing more to be made from the cotton gin. He'd managed to pay his debts, and that was all. He might do better on this new arms contract. Only time would tell. There was no use thinking now that there'd be money enough for a home and a family. Perhaps, some day, if he kept on . . .

Eli picked up his reins.

A long road yet.

"And a Bit of Earth"

⊏≣ IT HAD BEEN A BUSY DAY. THE third group of important visitors had just seen through the Whitney Armory. Eli walked outside with them to tell them good-by.

Almost closing time. He was glad. He was tired. Bone tired. He realized one of the visitors had said something to him.

Eli apologized. "I'm afraid my thoughts wandered."

The visitor chuckled. "Don't apologize, Mr. Whitney. That's a privilege of genius— to let your thought wander." Eli must have looked blank. The man said, "Don't you know you're a genius?"

Another of the visitors spoke up. "When a man does one thing that goes down in history, he's a genius. But you've done two. I don't know which will have more effect on the world—the cotton gin—or this system of making things by using uniform parts produced by machines."

The visiting delegation drove off. Eli stood a moment, looking off at the red cliffs that towered over Mill River.

"Some time, when I have time," he told himself, "I'll climb up there again and . . ."

From inside the armory he heard a crash and the shouts of his workmen. He hurried inside.

"It was Dumby," Tim Horner told him. "He was working on that new machine. I don't know how he did it, but the machine's wrecked."

Eli hurried to the huddle of men standing around the new machine. The man they called "Dumby" lay on the floor.

"What happened? How badly is he hurt?" Whitney knelt to examine the man. He could feel that the man's heart-beat was regular and he could find no broken bones.

A workman shrugged. "We didn't think he was hurt at all, Mr. Whitney. We heard the crash, and the machine stopped. I ran over. Dumby stared at me, wild-eyed. Like he was scared to death, and then he just went down in a heap. Fainted like!"

Eli, watching the man, saw his limbs trembling, saw his elbows draw against his sides. He seemed to be panic-stricken. What was the matter with him? No one could be that frightened over breaking a machine. It wasn't the first time something had been broken.

Eli said, "It's closing time. There's no need for the rest of you to wait around. I'll stay with the man and see that he gets home. Where does he live?"

There was no answer. Eli looked up. One after another, the men shrugged, shook their heads, and left the armory.

Tim Horner stayed. "You know how it is, Mr. Whitney. We don't know a thing about him. How could we? He'd never said a word. Just turned up here and made signs that he wanted to work. All we know is, that he comes in the morning, goes home at night, and is quick with his hands. I put him down on the pay roll as 'John Blank.' I had to call him something. But no one calls him that. Just 'Dumby.' Because he's never talked."

Eli looked down at the panic-stricken man. He felt his pulse. It was slow and regular. But his eyes were still closed. "So that's all we know. That he 'comes in the morning, goes home at night, and is quick with his hands.' How long has he been working for us?"

Tim counted up. "Let's see. . . . It's almost the end of June. About six months, I guess. He came around the first of the year. I know that war with England was still going on. He was here when we heard about Jackson winning the battle at New Orleans."

Under Eli's fingers, John Blank's pulse raced. His hands were trembling. He had heard the talk; he was listening. The war meant something to him, or England did.

Tim said, "Anyhow, that's how long he's been here. But I don't know where he lives."

Eli stood. "Well, if we don't know where he lives, I'll see that he's taken care of."

John Blank leaped from the floor and gripped Eli's arm. For the first time in all the months he spoke. "Please, Mr. Whitney! Please!" His voice was hoarse. It sounded like a string on a banjo that has grown rusty from disuse.

Tim gulped in bewilderment. "He can talk!"

John Blank shook Eli's arm. "Please, Mr. Whitney! It was an accident! Don't have me hanged for breaking the machine!"

Tim snorted. "Are you crazy? We don't hang men for breaking a machine."

Eli looked at the man. "You're English, aren't you?"

The man nodded. "You knew it the minute I opened my mouth. didn't you? That's why I never talked."

Tim said, "You poor stupid! What if you are English? Don't you know the war's over?"

John Blank didn't answer.

Eli thought of his fright, his frantic fear of being hanged. "John Blank, were you a Luddite?"

The man's face whitened. "No, no! I don't even know what you're talking about!"

"Don't you? Didn't you ever hear of Ned Ludd? He was an Englishman, a weaver, I believe. When weaving machines were invented and people were put out of work, Ned Ludd tried to destroy all the machines. You never heard of him?"

"No, no! I never did!" the rusty voice cried. "I'm not a Luddite! I never heard of them! I never broke into those factories at night to destroy machines. I never—" He realized he had said too much.

Eli said, "But someone you knew was a Luddite?"

"My father," he whispered numbly. "At first, he wasn't. But the men kept talking about how the machines took bread out of our mouths. If we destroyed all the machines, they said, we'd go back to the good old days. Humdrum days they were, with long hours and little food. But at least we didn't starve. My father went with the Luddite mob one time. Just once. He was caught."

"And hanged?"

John Blank nodded. "He was all the family I had. I was alone. When he was dead I ran away. I went to sea. When we got to America, I ran away from the ship. I thought I could start over, here."

Tim Horner sagged in a chair and rumpled

his hair. He hadn't known such things had happened when men invented machines.

Eli continued to question the man. "What made you want to work with machinery?"

John Blank shook his head. "I don't know, Mr. Whitney. I just don't know. Sometimes I hate it. Sometimes I love it. It's wonderful to see hundreds of little parts, made so fast, all perfect. But it does something queer to a man, Mr. Whitney. Seeing a machine do something you can't do, makes you feel like the machine was you and you were the machine." He looked up at Eli. "You wouldn't know about that, Mr. Whitney. Because you thought up the machine. You know you're the master."

Tim's voice was grim. "So you hate machines?"

John Blank turned pale. "I didn't mean to break the machine, Mr. Whitney."

"I believe you," Eli answered in a quiet voice.

"And you won't have me hanged? Or put in jail?"

"No."

"I'm free to go?"

Eli said, "Yes. Be here on time tomorrow."

John Blank stared. "I still have a job?"

Eli smiled wryly. "If I fired every man who broke something, I'd run out of workmen. Can you get home all right?"

"Oh, yes!" the man said hurriedly. "And I'll be here early tomorrow."

"Where do you live?" Whitney asked.

The man motioned with a hand that still trembled. "Clear on the other side of New Haven. It's just a little shack. But it's mine. I have my place, and a bit of earth." He smiled. "Does a man good to grow things, Mr. Whitney, after he's been with machines all day. Machines can't grow things."

When John Blank had gone, Eli walked outside and stared at the land that stretched away at the foot of the red cliffs.

"I wonder how much land I have here? I'll have to look it up."

Tim said, "Another building? A place for more machines?"

"No, Tim," Eli answered. And Tim knew by the far-away look in Whitney's eyes that he was thinking of the home he and Henrietta had just finished building. "A place for our workmen," Eli continued. "Good solid little homes. There's that money the state of South Carolina granted me 'for benefits received from the cotton gin.' I could use that."

South Carolina had made a payment of fifty thousand dollars for rights to Whitney's invention. It was rumored that North Carolina was going to pay something, too, and maybe Tennessee. But not Georgia — Georgia which had benefited most had offered no payment. Still, money was no longer a problem for Eli.

"Would you and Helen like a little home of your own out here?" Eli said. "Where you wouldn't have to go so far to your work?"

"Of course!" Tim's eyes were shining. "But —but—I mean—nobody's ever done anything like that! Built homes for his workmen!"

Eli grinned. "Does it sound fantastic? Just because it hasn't happened yet? You remember my definition of fantastic? I'm going to do it, Tim. Maybe it will give back to a man something the machine takes away. Maybe it will help a man to have a home of his own —and a bit of earth."

Long Courage

❧ IT WAS A DULL, QUIET SUNDAY afternoon. Tim Horner had fallen asleep in his highbacked, wooden chair. When a knock on the door wakened him, he opened one eye.

"Timmy! Hetty! One of you youngsters . . ." Then Tim remembered he was alone. Helen and the youngsters were away on a visit. He yawned and went to the door.

A tall, slender young Negro stood on the doorstep, with a portmanteau in one hand and a banjo in the other. He asked in a soft drawl, "Please, sir, which is Mr. Whitney's house?"

Tim rumpled his hair and looked at the

sturdy stone cottages all around him. "Well, you might say they're all Mr. Whitney's houses. He built them for his workmen."

The young man smiled eagerly, "Yes, sir. I heard about that! I've heard all about Mr. Whitney! My master, Mr. John Morrow, he talked about Mr. Whitney to his dying day! Which is Mr. Whitney's house?"

"He doesn't live here," Tim said. "He and Mrs. Whitney live in town, on Orange Street."

The young man snapped his fingers. "And I was just in New Haven! Reckon I walked right by that house coming out here!" He stepped back. "Thank you, sir. I'll—"

Tim said, "I think Mr. Whitney will be here after awhile. He said something about coming. Why don't you wait here for him? Come on in and have a cold drink with me. It's hot walking today."

When they were sitting in Tim's parlor, the young man showed Tim the letter he carried.

It was from Lucinda Morrow, widow of the late John Morrow. On John Morrow's death, Lucinda had freed all their slaves. Those who wished to, were staying at Pine Acres, to work for wages. Those who wished to settle elsewhere had been outfitted with clothes, and given money to help them travel and to tide them over while they got settled.

"I'm Cato," the young man said, "Young Cato. My pappy and my grandpappy belonged to Pine Acres. When my master died, men came and wanted to know did Miss Lucinda want to sell any of us. Miss Lucinda said *no*. She said she'd never see a human being bought or sold again. And she freed all of us, so, no matter what happened to her, we couldn't ever be bought and sold."

"How are things going at Pine Acres, with you people working for wages?" Tim asked.

Young Cato chuckled. "It's having its ups and downs. My Uncle Lycurgus, first time he get paid cash money, he spend it all *right then*. Then he go yelling to Miss Lucinda that he didn't want to be free. He didn't know how. Miss Lucinda, she tell him he'll learn. My pappy, now, he just pitch in and work twice as hard as he ever work in his whole life. So he get twice as much money as Uncle Lycurgus. He save it, too. So Uncle Lycurgus, he say that ain't fair."

Tim said, "It all sounds familiar. I remember the first time I ever had money of my own. I didn't have it long. I had to learn to handle money. Mrs. Morrow is right. A man has to

learn to handle anything new. Money or free-
dom or anything. And you decided you
wanted to come North?"

Young Cato nodded. "All my life I've heard
tell about Mr. Whitney. You see, once when
a load of cotton upset, Mr. Whitney, he
jumped off his horse and put his shoulder to
the wheel. And him, a white man and a
stranger. All my life I've heard about that.
So I thought I'd like to come and work for
Mr. Whitney."

There was another tap on the door. Tim
opened it to Henrietta and Eli and Young Eli,
the baby riding high on his father's shoulder.

After Eli had read Young Cato's letter and
made plans for him, they all went to the
armory.

It was an important visit for Young Eli,
Henrietta declared. After all, he was beginning
to teethe, and she thought he ought to have
something fitting to cut his teeth on. A cotton
gin was a little unwieldy; but perhaps a
musket . . .

Cato looked bewildered. Who ever heard
of a youngster cutting his teeth on a musket?
Then Eli Whitney threw back his head and
laughed, and Cato laughed, too.

Tim grinned. He felt as though his grin

began at his heels, and spread through him. Once he had thought Eli Whitney had missed everything. Now Eli Whitney had everything. It had been a long road. But Eli Whitney had had whatever it took to travel it. Tim wished he could put his finger on just what it was he wanted to say. . . .

The young Negro, Mrs. Whitney, and Tim stood together, watching Eli carry his young son through the armory.

As Eli paused by a high shelf, something bright caught the baby's eye. He lurched forward, grabbed with both hands, and tried to put his prize in his mouth.

Eli chuckled, and opened the little fist. The bright bit of metal was a hammer. A hammer that would fit any one of ten thousand muskets.

Tim said, "He's starting young!"

Eli Whitney was still smiling, but for a moment his eyes had a seeing-through-you look. "It's good to start young," he said. "It's a long road."

Tim found the word that he wanted to say. "And it takes long courage to travel it. That's it. Long courage."